Dear Pitman Publishing Customer

IMPORTANT – Please Read

We are delighted to announce a special free service fo

Simply complete this form and return it to the FREEPOST add

A   Free Customer Newsletter

B   Free Information Service

C   Exclusive Customer Offers – which have included free software, videos and relevant products

D   Opportunity to take part in product development sessions

E   The chance for you to write about your own business experience and become one of our respected authors

Fill this in now and return it to us (no stamp needed in the UK) to join our customer information service.

Name: _____   Position: _____

Company/Organisation: _____

Address (including postcode): _____

_____   Country: _____

Telephone: _____   Fax: _____

Nature of business: _____

Title of book purchased: _____

ISBN (printed on back cover): `0` `2` `7` `3` ☐ ☐ ☐ ☐   ☐

Comments: _____

-------------------- | Fold Here Then Staple Once | --------------------

We would be very grateful if you could answer these questions to help us with market research.

1   Where/How did you hear of this book?

☐ in a bookshop

☐ in a magazine/newspaper
(please state which):

_____

☐ information through the post

☐ recommendation from a colleague

☐ other (please state which):

_____

2   Where did you buy this book

☐ Direct from Pitman Publishing

☐ From a bookclub

☐ From a bookshop (state which)

_____

3   Which newspaper(s)/magazine(s) do you read regularly?:

_____

4   When buying a business book which factors influence you most?
(Please rank in order)

☐ recommendation from a colleague

☐ price

☐ content

☐ recommendation in a bookshop

☐ author

☐ publisher

☐ title

☐ other(s):

5   Is this book a

☐ personal purchase?

☐ company purchase?

**6   Would you be prepared to spend a few minutes talking to our customer services staff to help with product development?
YES/NO**

The Business Publisher

Written for managers competing in today's tough business world, our books will give you a competitive edge by showing you how to:

- increase quality, efficiency and productivity throughout your organisation
- use both proven and innovative management techniques
- improve your management skills and those of your staff
- implement winning customer strategies

In short they provide concise, practical information that you can use every day to increase the success of your business.

Free Information Service
Pitman Professional Publishing
FREEPOST
128 Long Acre
LONDON
WC2E 9BR, UK

No stamp
necessary
in the UK

A Practical Guide to
Solving Business Problems

■

A Practical Guide to Solving Business Problems

■

GEOF COX

the Institute
of Management
FOUNDATION

PITMAN
PUBLISHING

PITMAN PUBLISHING
128 Long Acre, London WC2E 9AN

A division of Pearson Professional Limited

First published in Great Britain 1995

British Library Cataloguing in Publication Data
A CIP catalogue record for this book can be obtained
from the British Library

ISBN 0 273 61182 8

1 3 5 7 9 10 8 6 4 2

Typeset by Northern Phototypesetting Co. Ltd, Bolton
Printed and bound in Great Britain by
Bell and Bain Ltd, Glasgow

*The Publishers' policy is to use paper manufactured
from sustainable forests.*

Contents

■

Acknowledgements

■

I am indebted to a number of people for the content of this book, both for their direct contribution and through their stories and reports that I have accumulated over the years. I thank them all for the material that they have, often unwittingly, provided.

Walt Hopkins was the first to develop my ideas with a practical application and has been a powerful source of inspiration in the development of the concepts in this book. He persuaded a number of organisations to run workshops based on these ideas whilst I was still trying to refine them in my own mind.

I am grateful to Professor Meredith Belbin and his publishers Butterworth Heinemann for permission to reprint the Self-Perception Inventory. Parts of chapter 13 first appeared in *Cuttings 9*, a news-letter published by Castle Consultants International.

Jeremy Kourdi at the Institute of Management expressed his belief in the idea from a very scrappy outline and Mark Allin at Pitman Publishing provided a challenging deadline that enabled me to focus on the end result.

My other colleagues at Castle Consultants International have been a source of ideas and support, especially Sheila Rimmer who has kept the business running during my absences.

Finally, I must apologise to my wife Joan and my daughter Kirsty for the interruption to our home and social life during the summer of writing.

Geof Cox
Castle Consultants International
21 Queen's Avenue
Edinburgh EH4 2DG

September 1994

Introduction

■

Problem solving is an activity that we all do every day, most of which is automatic. We have set up routines for ourselves to do things like get out of bed in the morning, take a shower, brush our teeth, get dressed, eat breakfast and go to work. In fact if you analyse each of these routines, you find a complex flowchart of sub-routines and decision points that start to overwhelm us. Each of these decision points is a problem to be solved – an opportunity to take in some information, weigh up consequences and alternatives and to choose a course of action. However, if we had to solve each of these problems from first principles each time, we would never get beyond the bathroom before it was time to go back to bed!

So our routines that have been born of experience are vital for us to survive. Without them we would never manage the complexity of life and work. But in these routines often lie the root cause of many of our difficulties. We set up routines to deal with different situations that are comfortable and suit our way of working. These routines work perfectly well when the environment and the situation remain the same, but when the environment changes for some reason, we are often thrown into a panic or a state of limbo. We find it difficult to make a decision as we are thrown out of our routine.

Most of the problems and situations we face are small and insignificant. It is quite easy to find an alternative to breakfast if the cereal box is empty. We develop a comfort with a particular approach to our environment. So some of us will prefer to have their clothes laid out in an orderly, prescribed manner and the table laid for breakfast before retiring to bed. Others of us will prefer an untidy house and the ability to choose what to eat and wear on the spur of the moment. We develop a preferred way of problem solving and decision making.

Once we have developed a preferred approach, we then try to use this approach and our routines in all situations that we encounter. This is often on the premise that what works in one situation may work in another – we might as well try the way we know first to see if it works. However, it may also be that we do not perceive any other approach and we keep on pursuing one method, even when it does not work, often not accepting the negative outcomes.

We also try to use our old routines to solve problems where the environment has changed. Many companies and organisations have carried through this process with devastating results, often going out of business or into deep recession as a result. The routines that brought success do not necessarily maintain success or guarantee success when the environment changes. Thus IBM had a very successful focus on the large, mainframe computers that they engineered to last. They noticed the personal computer threat rather late because their focus was on the mainframe market, not on the growing development of small, personal computers. On entering the market late, they quickly developed a dominance through their size of market and customer base, only to almost destroy the whole company a few years later. One of the contributing factors to their growing problems in the late 1980s and early 1990s was that they had over-engineered their personal computers. They had applied their old skills of mainframe engineering to the personal computer and designed a PC that would last for 25 years, when the actual life expectancy was 3 to 5 years. They used their old routines for problem solving in an environment that had changed, and was changing too rapidly for their processes to adapt.

Professor Reg Revans, the doyen of Action Learning, was fond of describing the current situation as 'living on the edge of a precipice'. The rate of pace of change in today's environment is so great that to only look backwards to history for data and information on which to make decisions is not sufficient. The information that we gather is inappropriate and out of date as the environment and circumstances have changed, even in the time it took to gather it. We need to collect information about the present and the future as well in order to make a balanced decision that is relevant to the current circumstances. Otherwise we are just walking backwards into the future.

So that we do not fall into the same trap as IBM, as organisations and as individuals, we need to be aware of the routines that we have developed. We need to understand the preferences that we have for solving problems and making decisions and for how we approach situations. We need to use a problem solving approach that values routines and past experience whilst scanning the current and future environment for opportunities and alternatives. We need to develop our skills and abilities to utilise the processes and people that we interact with to the best advantage so that we work at maximum effectiveness.

This book is about understanding yourself and valuing others. It will help you to analyse your own personal preferences, both in your approach to life and work, and in the way you like to interact when in a group or team. It will present a balanced approach to problem solving that will enable you to make the best use of the people and resources available to make effective decisions. Through case studies of organisations and situations, the book investigates some of the benefits and pitfalls of different approaches, and applies the balanced process to a number of common business and personal situations. The case studies are drawn from real life, but in some cases the names or situations have been changed to protect commercial confidence.

The book is practical and useful, and a number of exercises and activities are suggested that will allow you to apply the theories and ideas expounded on the pages to the real life situations that surround you and draw on the further examples that exist in your own experience. The book also introduces a number of tools and techniques that allow you, or your organisation, to compensate for the preference bias and to help in balancing your problem solving approach.

I hope that it provides the stimulus to think about your own approaches and prejudices and to value others' inputs and perceptions more. We cannot exist in the future without increasing levels of co-operation. This book is a small step in promoting this co-operation and the achievement of our futures, whatever they might be.

Personal style

We are all different from each other. Each person has a unique personality and set of preferences that affect the way in which we look at the world, take in information, process that information and make judgements. The set of preferences that make up our individual way of working has a profound effect on the way in which we approach problems, make decisions and carry them out. Understanding these preferences, our personal style, is an essential first step in improving our decision making and problem solving activity. In this chapter you will find a number of descriptions and activities that will help you to recognise both your own personal style and the basis of the differences that you have with other people.

Jung and others

What makes people different from each other has taxed the theorists and academics for centuries. Many different theories and ideas abound, and many tests are used (and misused) by organisations trying to get the right match of individual to the job. Many of these tests and instruments are based on the work of Carl Jung in the 1920s, as it seems that his approach to personality is more applicable to and has received more acceptance in the business world than some other theories.

Jung based his ideas on both observations of his clients in his psychoanalysis practice, and on evidence from the analysis of cultures and actions in history and his current environment. His observation was that there were a number of basic instincts or drivers for action within us, all of which are of equal importance. It is the combination of our preferences of these drivers that determines how we function and therefore what shape our personality takes. Given that there are groupings of preferences, Jung was able to categorise them into 'psychological types' giving a common language that can be used in making comparisons and understanding different behaviours and actions.

In the 1950s, a mother and daughter team of Katherine Briggs and Isabel Briggs-Myers re-visited the Jungian types and developed an instrument that could be used to identify these different patterns of action in individuals – the Myers-Briggs Type Indicator, or MBTI. This instrument is extensively used in the business world and is a major contributor to the development of individuals and organisations through its analysis of the different contributions made by members of the organisation. The measurement of your personal style in this chapter uses the research work and typology of the Myers-Briggs Type Indicator.

Different styles

We are all different. Just as we all have different facial features, different shoe sizes and different handwriting, so we also have differences in the internal motivators or drivers that make up our personality. Just as there is no 'correct' shoe size, and one style of handwriting is no more right than another, so there is no 'right' personality. What is important is that you know the shape and size of your own body so that you can buy the sort of clothes that suit and fit you. In the same way, it is important to know the shape and size of our personal style so that we can better understand the activities and approaches that fit us best.

The best way to discover your own preference and style is to take a Myers-Briggs Type Indicator test. This can only be administered by a qualified person, and you will receive a full description of your style and its implications. These tests are usually administered on a workshop or training course where the full benefits of the instrument are gained through the extra group discussion sessions and ability to compare results with other participants.

In the context of this book, it is not possible to reproduce the Myers-Briggs test, but a self-assessment of your preferences will assist you in understanding yourself and your interactions. Look at the descriptions listed in Table 1.1. The eight different traits are grouped in four sets of pairs. Each pair is composed of two extremes. In between these extremes there is a continuum of options. Very few people will associate only with one of the extreme descriptions in each pair, but we will feel more comfortable with one of the descriptions.

Identify for yourself where on the continuum you place yourself. If possible, ask colleagues or friends to identify how they see you operating, and compare their judgement with your own. This way you can

Table 1.1

YOUR PREFERRED PERSONAL STYLE

Look at each of the four pairs of descriptions in the table. Each pair describes an element of a personal style of working. The descriptions are the extreme points on a continuum where the centre marks a balance between the two opposing views. Choose a point on the continuum that reflects the strength of your preference for one statement over the other.

E   **I**

You actively seek the company and opinions of others are sensitive to their expectations	You prefer personal reflection and are sensitive to your own beliefs and values

S   **N**

You pay attention to facts and to specific and practical information	You pay attention to ideas, images, dreams and possibilities for the future

T   **E**

Your decisions are made by logical analysis based on objective criteria	Your decisions are made by considering beliefs, values and relationships

J   **P**

You prefer to make quick decisions and close things down	You prefer to keep options open and resist closure

build up a body of evidence on how you see yourself and how others see you. (Other people are often better at observing our behaviour than we are ourselves.)

Interpreting the results

The initial letters on each end of the scale in Table 1.1 are the usual way of representing each of the eight traits. Take the letter nearest the point where you have marked your position on the scale. The initial letters from the four scales will give you a four letter code, such as ESTJ, INFP, ENFJ, etc. These four letter codes identify which of the sixteen different 'types' characterises your behaviour.

Remember, there are no right and wrong answers. Jung and his later followers are not saying that you are only one thing or the other. In some cases we will operate in one way, in other situations we will follow a different set of actions. But overall, we will have a strength of preference for one set of actions over the other. The type descriptions mark the extreme positions at the end of a continuum. We are all somewhere in the middle, with a tendency to prefer one side or the other. It is this overall preference that sets our 'normal' pattern of behaviour.

The stronger your attraction to one statement rather than the other indicates the strength of your preference for one trait over the other. The more you favour one way, the less you value and understand the opposite viewpoint. The nearer your preference to the centre point, the more you are able to move your actions and behaviour between the two traits and the more you can accept and value the different approaches. Neither position is better than the other.

The strength of our preferences may also change over time, depending on the situations we face and the information we have. What is important is that the typology gives us a way of comparing how and why people differ in their actions. It is a snapshot of your current personal style. In later discussion in this book, we will investigate the implications of your preferred style in making decisions, and the implications for organisations and groups in having people of similar or different preferences.

The four pairs of preferences

The E-I pair: Extroversion (E) – Introversion (I)

The distinction between extroversion and introversion in the context of the Type characteristics is different from the common usage of the words extrovert and introverts. We often load these terms with stereotypes, seeing extroverts as friendly, outgoing people and introverts as hermits and social misfits. While some of this stereotyping may be true, there are many introverts who mix well, and many extroverts who lack even the basic social skills. The definitions of extroversion and introversion in the Jungian typology are much more fundamental. They relate to our perception of the world and where we find our source of energy.

Extroversion means that you pay attention to the outer world rather than the inner. Your source of energy derives from interaction with others. Even when an extrovert has had a tiring day dealing with people, she or he will seek out the company of other people in order to energise themselves again. Extroverts need to find out what other people and society thinks and what it expects of them so that they can fit their actions to those expectations.

5

Introversion, on the other hand, means that you pay attention to your inner voice, and focus on your own beliefs and values more than the opinions and expectations of others. When an introvert needs to recharge her or his batteries, solitude and reflective thought does the trick. Introverts will want to step back and think about what things mean to them and to decide a course of action that fits with their own values.

It follows from these two extreme orientations that a number of typical actions and behaviour patterns can be added to each type. Someone with a tendency to extroversion will find it easy to talk to people about their own and others' thoughts and feelings; they look for breadth of information and will have a number of relationships. Even when confronted by the impersonal world of the electronic office, an extrovert will develop a series of networks to enable her or him to communicate with others, and will use the technology to build new contacts and opportunities.

Someone with an introversion tendency will be reluctant to share information about their thoughts and feelings. They will tend to look for depth of information and limit their relationships to a small number of trusted people. When in groups and social situations, an introvert will often find her or his own personal space by concentrating on internal conversations and reflection rather than engaging in 'small talk.'

If you have chosen extroversion as your preferred style, then you are in common with the majority. In studies, three-quarters of the general population show a tendency to extroversion, only one quarter reporting introversion as their preference. With such a large proportion of the population having a tendency to one trait, the possibility of misunderstanding the other is greatly enhanced. Those in the minority undoubtedly feel pressure to conform to what is seen to be 'normal' behaviour patterns rather than follow their own preferred style.

The S-N pair: Sensing (S) – Intuition (N)

The scope for misunderstanding that arises between those with extroversion and introversion preferences pales into insignificance when one analyses the differences in this pair of preferences. This pair provides the greatest source of difference between people and provides the greatest source of argument, misunderstanding and poor communication.

The Sensing – Intuition pair measure our preference for how we take in information; how we perceive the world around us.

If your preference is to the sensing end of the spectrum, then you are expressing a desire to take in information through your senses. You pay attention to information that you can see, feel, hear, taste, touch and smell. No other information has any validity because it does not exist. Yours is the world of facts and data, the world of practicality and objectivity, the world of historical and current information, the world of concrete experience.

If your intuition preference is stronger, then you tend to live in the world of the possible and the future. The information that you pay attention to is that which comes from relationships and meaning and speculation, from hypothesis and theory and vision. Factual information, as defined by a sensing person, is only important as a springboard to your imagination and as trigger to ask 'why?' and 'what if?' questions.

So, the sensing person deals in the here and now, the sensible and the practical. The intuitive person deals in the future, the possible and the innovative. There is a vast store of misunderstandings and miscommunications between these two preferences. Once again there is a population split of three-quarters to one-quarter, this time in favour of the sensing preference that compounds the possibilities for misunderstanding. Although we all use both processes some of the time, our preference to favour one over the other develops a comfort zone around that style and a lack of appreciation of the value of the other.

The T-F pair: Thinking (T) – Feeling (F)

The sensing – intuition pair measures our preference for taking in information, the thinking – feeling pair measures our preference for processing that information. Thinking and feeling are two different ways of making judgements about the perceptions we have. A person who prefers to make decisions in an impersonal way has a thinking style. A person who prefers a personal basis for their decisions has a feeling style. Both approaches are useful and valid. It is a matter of personal preference which is the more comfortable for you, and a function of the situation which is the most appropriate and effective.

If you have a preference to the thinking process then you value logical analysis and rational decision making. Whether or not the information is perceived through sensing or intuition, the thinker will weigh the evidence and think rationally about the conclusions. Thinkers set up systems for decision making that they can use in many situations.

A feeling preference means that you tend to make decisions based on values and beliefs and will probably express these decisions by using words such as 'ought' and 'should.' Processing information in a feeling way is not necessarily emotional, though relationships and personal feelings are important. It is more of a process that decides a 'right' way based on a set of values and beliefs.

We are all capable of using both processes, and can usually appreciate the benefits of each. The Western education system tends to favour the thinking approach as does much of our established business and organisational life. There is therefore a tendency to overplay the logical, rational approach and use it in inappropriate situations.

The general population split is 50:50 between the two preferences, though there is a gender difference. In studies, 60 per cent of females express a tendency to the feeling process and 60 per cent of males express a tendency for the thinking process. This has led to a number of stereotypes and miscommunications based on a female, or soft way of making decisions against a male, or hard way of making decisions. These gender labels are not useful except to highlight the other approach, as there are significant minorities of each gender who express a preference for the other process. However, as we will discover in later chapters, it is the grouping of like minds together that will cause deeper problems, both in making effective decisions and in understanding and valuing the opposite preference.

The J-P pair: Judging (J) – Perceiving (P)

This pair of traits measures the preference we have to how we approach decisions. Do you prefer to close things down or keep things open and fluid? Do you prefer outcomes or the process itself? Do you want to make a decision and move on quickly to the next one, or do you want to gather more data and develop more options?

If you have a tendency to close down, take quick, decisive action and to take interest in the outcome, then you have a preference for the judging process. Judging people make quick decisions, on the basis of whatever data is available at the time. They rarely change a decision once made, whether it is found to be right or wrong, preferring to move on to the next decision and outcome that is needed.

A perceiving tendency means that you are more interested in the process, in data collection, than you are in the outcome or decision. You will tend to resist closure and avoid making decisions in favour of collecting more information and developing further options. Flexibility is important, as is being open and non-judgemental. You are willing to reconsider decisions at any time in the light of new evidence.

There seems to be an equal population split between those with a judging preference and those with a perceiving preference, though in organisations and working groups, the selective employment process of recruiting in your own image will distort this balance, making the scope for misunderstanding even greater. Even without this extra source, the difference between those who want to make decisions and those who want to search for more data or opinions is a major cause of disputes and misunderstanding.

Your own preference

On the basis of what you have read, go back to Table 1.1 and reconsider the decision that you made on your personal style preferences.

What is your reaction to that suggestion?

If you feel that you would like to gather more data and make some changes then you are demonstrating a Perceiving preference. If you

Table 1.2

SUMMARY OF THE STYLE CHARACTERISTICS

Preferred perception of the world

Extraversion	**Introversion**
Outer world.	Inner voice.
Energy from interaction with others.	Energy from within.
Need to know what others expect.	Focus on our own beliefs and values.
Adapt actions to those expectations.	Action determined by own values.
Many relationships.	Few relationships.
Breadth of information.	Depth of information.

Preferred way of taking in information

Sensing	**Intuiting**
Information from the senses.	Information from speculation and
Facts and data.	theory.
Practical and realistic.	Broad principles and ideas.
Present time.	Interest in the possible.
Concrete experience.	Future orientation.
	Innovation.

Preferred way of processing information

Thinking	**Feeling**
Logical analysis.	Subjective.
Rational decision making.	Decisions based on values and beliefs.
Systems, rules and procedures.	Relationships.
Impersonal.	Personal.

Preferred approach to decision making

Judging	**Perceiving**
Close down.	Resist closure.
Quick, decisive action.	Avoid making decisions.
More interested in outcomes.	More interested in process.
Consider available data.	Collect more data and options.
Rarely change a decision.	Flexible and adaptive.
Organise and plans.	Lets things happen.

have a desire to move on and stick by the analysis you made earlier, then that demonstrates that you are more likely to have a preference for Judging.

Some of you will want to collect more specific data. You feel uneasy with the subjective nature of the theory and want to get some hard concrete facts that will demonstrate whether it is worthwhile spending further time on the subject. You are showing a strong Sensing tendency. On the other hand, an Intuiting preference will gather the general concepts and will be speculating on the preferences of colleagues, friends and family and will already have been seeing some of the implications for relationships and the future.

Some of you will be wanting to question the statistical validity of the instruments and wish to follow up references and research to understand the rules and categories used. You have a preference for Thinking. Others will be balancing the values and ideas expounded here to their own internal model of the world and deciding the circumstances for using the theory in improving harmony and understanding in relationships. You are using your Feeling approach to analysing the data.

Pay attention to your reactions – your first response is usually a good guide to your real preference.

The sixteen types

Based on different combinations of these four pairs of preferences, there are sixteen possible personal styles.

Read the profile for your own preferred style. Look at those where you have a close relationship, for instance if your preference is for ESTJ but your strength of preference was very small on the T-F and J-P pairs, then read the descriptions for ESFJ, ESFP and ESTP as well as your primary preference for ESTJ. You will probably recognise some characteristics of your behaviour and personal style in each of these descriptions. Finally, look at your opposite. In the case of ESTJ this would be INFP. Notice how easy it is to relate to the descriptions that are close to yours and how hard it is to associate with your opposites.

It is these differences in personal style that cause many disagreements and arguments in the home, the workplace and in social situations. People just see the world from different perspectives and think differently.

Table 1.3

THE SIXTEEN STYLES

ISTJ	ISFJ	INFJ	INTJ
Decisive. Quiet and serious. Dependable and loyal. Practical, thorough. Handles detail and routine well. Patient.	Dependable, traditionalist. Values established routines. Good at following tasks through. Help others. Loyal.	Focused on possibilities. Take work seriously. Empathy for others. Enjoy problem solving	Self-confident. Designer f models and systems. Natural brainstormer. Single minded. Can be cold and dispassionate.
ISTP	**ISFP**	**INFP**	**INTP**
Active. Practical Good at using tools and machines. Poor communicators. Impulsive. Self-directed.	Active, sympathetic, sensitive to others. Reserved and private. Seeks freedom and excitement.	Calm. Idealistic. Loyal to causes and people. Prefers values to logic. Adaptive, innovative.	Precise. Quick to identify contradiction Good theorist. Designs systems and ideas, rarely implements them.
ESTP	**ESFP**	**ENFP**	**ENTP**
Action oriented. Entrepreneurial. Trouble-shooter. Good sales people. Poor at follow through.	Optimistic, warm, generous. Prefer to be active. Poor at working alone. Relies heavily on personal experience.	Easily bored. Avoids routine. Seeks opportunities for creativity Enthusiastic and innovative.	Sensitive to possibilities. Good analysts. Have an eye for a new way. Innovative. Non-conformist.
ESTJ	**ESFJ**	**ENFJ**	**ENTJ**
Focus on outside world. Organising Evaluative. Expect people to run to standard procedures and rules. Practical.	Sociable. People focused. Outgoing. Promote harmonious relationships. Practical and loyal. Clear values.	Good leaders of groups. People are a high priority, relate to others well. Effective verbal communicators.	Strong drive to lead. Structured, organised planners. Intolerant of inefficiency. Demand order and support from others

Strengths and weaknesses

Most of us view our preferred style as a strength. We are probably in a role where the particular characteristics of our style are of value, and we relate easily to our colleagues and friends who are of a similar make-up. When confronted with someone who thinks or behaves differently to our norm, we tend to dismiss their actions as odd and return to our comfort zone of similar thinkers as quickly as possible.

The paradox is that the strengths we often perceive in our own style can also be weaknesses, especially when they are carried to an extreme. As in many things, overuse of a strength can turn it into a weakness.

Extroverts find their strengths in working in groups and being able to communicate freely and openly with other people. They focus on the outer world, tending to follow group values and carry out actions that have the approval of others. These behaviours provide the strength of conformity and sociability, but can also mean that extroverts are easily distracted and waste time on trivial discussion. Their desire for acceptance can lead to carrying out poor decisions and 'group-think' where no one speaks out on a subject known to be wrong because everyone believes that they all know about it.

Introverts are independent thinkers and take time to think about the consequences of their actions before embarking on a course of action. They therefore appear as slow and reserved. They often will avoid group activities and ignore outside influences and events. The strength of concentration that allows them to work in isolation for long periods of time also makes them intolerant of interruptions and a source of mistrust.

The strength of a sensing preference is in the attention to detail and the ability to apply experience to current situations. This attention to detail leads to people getting bogged down and not being able to 'see the wood for the trees', missing the overall picture in a situation. Relying too much on experience will mean that the opportunity to try out new or innovative solutions is missed and much activity will be carried out 'because we have always done it that way'.

Intuitors often find their strengths in innovation and the ability to see possibilities and options. They can scan the environment quickly for information on which to base their thinking. However, this can mean that they miss relevant facts and ignore obstacles, wasting their own and everyone else's time on impractical ideas. Intuitors are often so fascinated by the novel and the new that they totally ignore existing and sound processes and procedures just because they are not new. Much time and money were wasted during the early developments of information technology when intuitors were finding ever more possibilities for automating processes that were more efficient and effective when being carried out manually.

The obvious strength of a Thinking preference is in the analytical and objective approach to problem solving. The use of systems and procedures are second nature to a thinker, as is the development of standard operating procedures and models for understanding operations. This impersonal approach is often seen as cold and calculating. Not all problems lend themselves to logical and analytical processes, and thinkers find it impossible to understand the reactions of others to their lack of consideration of people's feelings.

On the other hand, those with a Feeling preference are very people oriented and can become so involved in the relationship and emotional side of an issue that they often overlook or ignore the task needs. Their strength is in understanding relationships and the needs of others, but they can easily turn this empathy to misplaced sympathy, over-dramatising events and attributing feelings and emotions inappropriately.

Judging has its strength in the ability to make quick decisions, cutting through the data to get down to basics and work methodically to a plan. The strength becomes a weakness when the speed of decision making leaves out relevant data and the need to make a decision is seen as more important than making the right decision. Very often judgers have made a decision based on inadequate data that is subsequently proved to be less than perfect – they then compound the problem by sticking to their original position in the light of new data. Confidence and decisiveness have become inflexibility and dogma.

The strength of perceiving is to consider all sides of the situation and collect all forms of opinion and data before making a quality judgement, then remaining flexible enough to change that decision in the light of new evidence. Thus perceivers often miss deadlines and often seem to collect data and opinions that are not relevant to the subject in hand. They may even take their flexibility to such an extreme that they are unable to make any decision at all, or vacillate between different positions causing confusion and anxiety in those who are trying to carry out the actions.

Balanced perception

So by just relating to one view of the world – our own preferred style – we can overplay our strengths to the detriment of ourselves and our organisation and we miss out on a large amount of information and perceptions that could be useful to us. The answer is to try to balance our viewpoint by learning to value and take notice of our opposites.

As we found earlier, this will be easier to do the closer we relate to the two preference choices. The further along the continuum towards the extreme that we find ourselves, the harder it is to understand the other preference, let alone make use of the different information available from that perspective or value the difference. Consider the following statements as a start to the process of balancing your perception of the world and to making better decisions:

Extroverts can use Introversion to help them to discover their own values and beliefs and use them to make their own judgement instead of just following the group norms.

Introverts can use Extroversion to test their own values and beliefs in the wider context of the outer world rather than only considering one viewpoint.

Sensers need to balance their factual data collection with an Intuitor's ability to see possibilities, patterns and relationships within the data that will lead to innovation and breakthrough.

Intuitors need to balance their imagination with a Sensing approach that keeps a focus on reality and stops them jumping to conclusions based on insufficient or inaccurate data.

Thinkers can benefit from considering information from a Feeling perspective in order to consider the wider issues and relationships before making decisions, especially where there are people implications.

Feelers can benefit from considering information from a Thinking perspective in order to put some logic and rationality into their arguments, especially where they are dealing with issues that are not people related.

Judgers need Perceiving skills to slow down their decision making and make quality decisions based on sufficient information; to be more flexible and less dogmatic.

Perceivers need Judging skills to help them to make decisions and to keep to plans and deadlines; to take action and get organised.

Problem solving and decision making

It is clear from the above analysis that our own personal style has a strong effect on the quality of our problem solving and decision making. If we are working alone, then our personal style preference will guide our approach. So if our style was ISTJ, then we will approach the problem on our own through systematic and thorough analysis, using logical analysis of the available data gained from tangible experience, and

14

take decisive action, regardless of protests. By contrast, someone with an ENFP style would approach the problem in an enthusiastic, almost inspiring manner, focusing on possibilities and coming up with original and creative ideas.

Our own style is successful, but there is a danger, as we saw in the earlier analysis, that our strength can become our weakness. There is definite benefit in trying to balance our decision making by thinking of the other perceptions, taking in as much different information as possible, and then taking action on the basis of a higher quality decision.

The uneven distribution of the population especially between sensing and intuiting types and the focus of our education and business system on logical and rational analysis causes us to have developed a skewed value system that tends to treat ST approaches as normal and looks with suspicion on anyone with an N or an F tendency. Those who have the latter preferences have been under attack for their thinking for so long that they often feel more inclined to defend their position than to understand the difference. Only by working hard to look for the positive features on both sides will we be able to overcome our prejudice and to benefit from the total perception of the problem.

In later chapters, the need for balance and further implications of our personal preferences are further discussed, along with organisational case studies of success and failure that highlight the strengths and weaknesses of different approaches. In the next chapter, we look at the problem solving process and our preferences for different styles when working in a group.

Summary

We each have a personal preference to the way we approach the world, take in information, process that information and make decisions. Based on this preference we have a strong tendency to associate with people who think and behave like us, and to disassociate with and mistrust those who think and behave differently. However, what we perceive as the strength of our own approach, and that of our colleagues, may well be a weakness when it is over-played. Our personal style affects the way we approach and solve problems, and we can miss out on over three-quarters of the valid information available on which to base our decisions due to our own bias and preference. The most effective problem solving comes from trying to balance our preferred approach with those who think differently – pooling our strengths and coming up with a new strength that is the combination of both.

2

Working in a team

As well as having a personal style of working, we each have a preferred way of working when we are part of a team. Many of us have experienced being in a successful team at some time in our lives, being part of a unified, productive and fun unit. We have also probably experienced being in an unsuccessful group, where the people did not seem to gel, where individuals pursued their own interests and frequently clashed with other group members.

We have all met some different types of people in teams, or worked with them – the steady plodder, the person who is constantly questioning ideas, the driving force, the ideas person, the person who is always staying late to finish the last piece of the report. Individually, they may drive us mad, but put them together in a team, and they can achieve high performance. Rather than trying to knock each other out, they concentrate their effort and knock out the opposition. The key is to recognise that each of these types, or roles that people take on in a team, are vital to the success of the team. No role is more important than any other, in fact it is the balanced team with a mix of all roles that produces the most spectacular results.

Research carried out by Dr Meredith Belbin[1] in the 1970s, predominantly at the Management College, Henley, identified that all members of a management team have a dual role. There is the obvious functional role that the person fulfils as a member of the team – sales manager, accountant, production head, service engineer, data processing manager, or whatever. But it is the second role that is crucial when it comes to effectiveness. This is the role that individuals take on in determining how the team works, rather than the content of the work itself – the team role.

Tom keeps coming up with bright ideas, Dick wants to get things decided and moving, and Harriet is always tying up the loose ends.

---

[1] R. Meredith Belbin, *Management Teams – Why They Succeed or Fail*, Heinemann, 1981

They exhibit these characteristics in every team that they are in – the product development project team, the committee of the dramatic society, or the governors of the local school. If we could identify the team roles we prefer to follow, and use them to play off against each other and balance each other, then we have the makings of success. Only a team that understands itself has the opportunity to reap the benefits of the hundreds of per cent improvements in productivity that are possible from high performance teams.

Your own team role

Have a look at the behaviour descriptions in Table 2.1. They are in eight groups that relate to the behaviours most associated with the eight most important team roles. Read through these now and decide which of the eight most describes how you prefer to operate in a team? Get others who work with you or know you to look at this table and identify the role that they observe you performing. This will give you a comparison to make with your own perception.

When you have identified your preferred role from Table 2.1, identify the role name from Table 2.2. Then read on, looking at the description of your own role and those of the other seven team roles. If others have identified different roles for you from their observations, then pay particular attention to these differences when reading through the role descriptions. Try to identify where your colleagues could see you using that behaviour in a team, and whether you behave differently in different teams. This will help your understanding of how you work when in a team situation.

In Appendix 1 at the end of the book, a self-perception Inventory will give you a more accurate assessment of your team role preferences. As well as identifying your main preferences, it also identifies where you have specific weaknesses and gaps that can cause problems in effective teamwork and problem solving. You will find it useful to complete the inventory, especially when working through the later chapters in the book.

Table 2.1

	ROLE BEHAVIOUR
A	• I like to organise and plan action steps using practical common sense. • I work hard. • I understand and use systems that get things done. • I can carry out plans before they have been fully developed.
B	• I like to keep the focus on the objective. • I involve everyone in the task. • I often ask people to do things that I could do myself. • I sometimes abdicate in the face of powerful competition.
C	• I drive the team to achieve results. • I challenge inertia, ineffectiveness, complacency, time wasting and majority views. • I sometimes use my role to promote myself. • I will compete with other team members for leadership.
D	• I am the primary source of creativity, imagination, ideas and original approaches. • I ignore the obvious and focus on possibilities. • I often take offence when my ideas are evaluated or rejected. • I do not enjoy carrying out tasks.
E	• I find information and resources from outside the team. • I like to propose how to take advantage of new opportunities. • I instinctively build up contacts outside the team. • I tend to get bored when involved in routing work.
F	• I provide critical judgement to the team's work. • I analyse situations for all the possible problems and opportunities. • I stay cool under pressure. • I can be tactless and destructive in criticising others suggestions.
G	• I like to relate to people personally and promote team spirit. • I work well with a wide range of people. • I support the ideas of others. • I can let good feelings get in the way of completing the task.
H	• I finish any task that I, or the team, begin. • I can prevent careless mistakes from spoiling the success of a project. • I put my full attention to completing a task. • I often focus on the urgent rather than the important.

Table 2.2

A	IMPLEMENTER
B	COORDINATOR
C	DRIVER
D	CREATOR
E	INVESTIGATOR
F	EVALUATOR
G	COMMUNICATOR
H	FINISHER

The team roles

Coordinator

You are the person who presides over the team and co-ordinates its efforts to meet goals and targets, though you are not necessarily in the position of the leader of team. You are often preoccupied with objectives and have an approach well founded in self-discipline. You are relaxed, not domineering, but have a strong and pre-eminent position in the team.

You tend to focus on what people in the team do best, trying to use the combined human resource as effectively as possible. You will establish the task roles and work boundaries of others in the team and take steps to fill any gaps that you perceive, either by taking on the role yourself, or by recruiting new members to the team.

You are a good communicator, talking easily, and being easy to talk to, and being a good listener. You clarify the team's objectives, set its agenda, and establish its priorities. In the early stages of team development, your contributions are likely to be questions rather than proposals or assertions. You will then listen actively to the responses, sum up group feelings, articulate group verdicts, and take decisions when needed after everyone has had their say. In most respects you act as the chairman, albeit often informal, of the group.

When you are under stress, your behaviours tend to harden and you exhibit rigidity and obstinacy, often not recognising ability and merit in the team, or not using all possible team resources. You will often refuse to admit the superior ability in other team members, and compete with others. In the face of powerful competition, usually from Drivers, you often abdicate your role.

As a manager or leader, you can employ your talents overtly. However, you should always remembering that effective team performance is the objective. You must be prepared to shift between taking a leading role, and using the complimentary talents of others according to the situation and resources.

Driver

The Driver, as the role name suggests, drives the team's efforts. You are the self-appointed task leader of the team, and you are likely to be the actual leader in the absence of a Coordinator, or where the Coordinator is not appointed as the formal leader. You are full of energy, impatient, easily frustrated, quick to challenge, and equally quick to respond to a challenge. You often have conflicts and arguments with other team members, but they are usually over quickly, and you do not harbour grudges. However, you need to be aware that other team members may resent your drive and not forgive or forget as quickly.

You invest a lot more of your own personal feelings and desires than the Coordinator, who tends to be more objective. In discussions you try to unite ideas into a single project that you can then push forward urgently to decision and action.

You want action, and you want it now. You are personally competitive, intolerant of vagueness and muddled thinking, and are often described as arrogant and abrasive. Team members are in danger of being steam-rollered on occasions, making the team atmosphere uncomfortable. In the absence of strong team members in other roles, you can easily manipulate the team to pursue courses of action that support your own personal objectives and direction rather than the team's. Like Margaret Thatcher in her Cabinet, you drive through your own policies and demand support, systematically eliminating any dissension. There is certainly no room for more than one Driver in a team.

You are best when operating in a team of peers. In a formal leadership position, you need to watch for and to avoid the tendency to be insensitive to the other team members with an attitude that only your decisions count.

Creator

Belbin gave the name 'Plant' to this role, as he found one of the best ways to improve a team's performance was to 'plant' one of these people into the group. You can also be seen as the person who scatters the seeds for others to nurture, you are the ideas person, the source of original suggestions and proposals.

What distinguishes your ideas from others is their originality. Your radical approach to problems means that you are the most likely to bring new insight to a line of action. However, you are often so concerned with major issues, that you miss some detail and make careless mistakes.

Whilst you tend to introversion, you can also be very forthright and can easily cause offence to others when criticising their ideas. But the main danger for the team is that you will devote too much energy to ideas that do not fall within the team's needs or objectives. And you are certainly not especially interested in putting any of your ideas into action. Your satisfaction comes with the creative activity not the implementation.

If criticised or confronted you have a tendency to withdraw and take offence. Even though you may have a very useful contribution to make to the process or task, you will refrain from doing so in the fear of rejection. Despite all of these faults, you provide the vital spark in the team.

If you should hold a managerial or leadership role, you must exercise considerable self-discipline and be prepared to listen to your team's comments on proposals and ideas (particularly those from the Evaluator member(s)). Failure to do this can soon take the team in inappropriate directions with disastrous results. The stresses of controlling a team can stifle creative output, so you must always keep your role objective in mind.

Evaluator

By contrast with other team roles, Evaluators are serious and not very exciting. But it is your measured, dispassionate analysis and monitoring that provides the team with the perfect balance to the onslaught of originality from Creators or the unfettered enthusiasm of Drivers. The very successful teams form these alliances consciously.

Although a critic by nature, you do not usually criticise for the sake of it, but only where you can see a flaw in the plan or argument. You have the most objective mind in the team; personal ego does not cloud or distort the slow, methodical process of your judgement.

Your most valuable skills are in assimilating, interpreting, and evaluating large volumes of complex written material, and analysing and assessing the judgements and contributions of the other team members. Unfortunately, sometimes this analysis and assessment is tactless, which means that you will rarely win a popularity contest, especially when you apply the damper at the wrong time and lower the team morale.

You are solid and dependable, fair-minded and objective, though often lacking in warmth, imagination and spontaneity. Your judgement is hardly ever wrong, and that is your greatest value to the team performance.

Under stress, you have a tendency to use your own critical thinking ability for personal advantage, at the expense of team objectives. You can also lower the team morale by being over-critical and showing negative thinking. When you are also the manager or leader of a team, you must take extra care not to over-dominate the other members of the team with your highly developed critical thinking ability.

Implementer

You are the practical organiser, turning the decisions and strategies into defined and manageable tasks that people can get on with. You are concerned with what is feasible, converting the team's plans into a practical form, sorting out objectives, and pursuing them logically.

You are not easily deflated or discouraged, and only get upset when there is a sudden change of plan. You particularly dislike unstable, quickly changing conditions preferring to work with stable structures. Your need for order and stability is characterised by your continual review and building of new structures – turning decisions into schedules; people and objectives into organisation charts.

You tend to work efficiently, methodically and systematically, although sometimes inflexibly. You are close to being the team's fulcrum – if people do not know what has been decided and what is supposed to be done, they are likely to go to you first to find out.

Your main fault, which often shows up most when you are under pressure or in a management or leadership role, is an over-eagerness to carry out plans before they have been fully developed, favouring action above all else. You can also be over-critical on others ideas for lack of practical application.

Investigator

As the name implies, you are the member of the team who goes outside the group and brings back information, ideas and developments. Because you have an ability to stimulate ideas and encourage innovation through this contact with the world outside the team, you can be confused with the ideas role – Creators. However, you do not have the radical originality of Creators, the ideas are not your own but are taken from other situations and people and applied to the current team task.

You tend to be positive and enthusiastic, though prone to put things down just as quickly as they are picked up. You make friends and contacts easily. In fact, in a solitary job, without the stimulus of others, you can easily become bored, demoralised and ineffective. Within the team, however, you are a good improviser, active under pressure, but can over-relax when the pressure eases. A poor time manager, you can fail to follow up tasks undertaken in one of your frequent bursts of short-lived enthusiasm, and like Creators, spend too much time on irrelevancies.

Your most important team role is to preserve the team from stagnation and losing touch with reality, though you must balance this with a tendency to concentrate too much on the development of external contacts and pursuits at the expense of team membership and task completion.

23

Communicator

You are the most sensitive of the team – the most aware of individual's needs and worries, and the one who perceives most clearly the emotional undercurrents in the group. You are the most active internal communicator, the cement of the team. Your instinct is to build on other's ideas, rather than to demolish them or produce a rival idea.

You are a very willing communicator and listener, helping and encouraging others to do likewise. By promoting unity and harmonious relationships, you counterbalance the friction and discord that can be caused by Drivers, Creators and Evaluators. Having a dislike for personal confrontation you tend to try to head if off or cool it down.

It is when the team is under pressure or in difficulties that your role flourishes. By showing sympathy, understanding, loyalty and support, both on an individual and group basis you can prevent division and disruption in the team. In normal times the value of your individual contribution may not be as visible as the other team roles, but the when the team is in a time of stress and pressure, your absence is noted.

Finisher

You worry about what might go wrong, and are never at ease until you have personally checked every detail and made sure that everything has been done, and nothing has been overlooked.

You are not assertive, but maintain a permanent sense of urgency that is communicated to others to galvanise them into activity. You have a strict preoccupation with order, compulsively meeting deadlines and maintaining schedules. You are therefore impatient with, and intolerant of, the more casual and slap-happy team members.

You can have a lowering effect on the morale of the team by excessive worrying, can also lose sight of the overall objective easily by getting bogged down in details.

The relentless tendencies to follow-through and finish the team's activities are your most important assets.

24

The team as a whole

As you can see from reading all of the role descriptions, each of the roles has a real value to the successful working of the team, and the absence of any one of them weakens the team. Equally, the presence of too many of one type produces imbalances that can cause predictable failures: too many Creators will produce many ideas that are never taken up; too many Drivers will be constantly fighting for leadership and their own ideas.

One of the most important outcomes of the research was that the most successful teams are not the teams of similar characters, nor the teams of the most qualified or expert task people. They are those who have a balance of all eight roles represented in them. This balance is critical to the process of problem solving and decision making in team that we will investigate in later chapters.

Now you have identified your own role and obtained the input from others, reflect on what effect your role has on the effective working of a team. What is your experience of working in different teams? Have you behaved differently (which might indicate an ability to move between team roles easily depending on the situation), or has your behaviour always been the same (which indicates a very strong preference for a particular role, and a consequential inflexibility and intolerance of other roles).

Look critically at all of the role descriptions and identify those that you feel are less valuable than others. Which roles make you frustrated? (It is often useful to try to put a character that you know from business or public life into each of the roles to focus your feelings.) It is these roles that you need to learn to value more in the successful workings of the team. Look for the positive attributes of working with these people and their value in balancing the weaknesses of your own role. Remember that a weakness is most often an over-use of a strength.

Summary

Each of us has a preferred way of working when we operate in a group or team environment. This preferred role is carried with us from one team to another and is independent of the task role that we perform in a team. The research work carried out on team roles suggests that a team that has a balance of all eight roles in its make-up will outperform all other teams. It is therefore important to understand your own preference and the preferences of the other team members of all of your teams whether at work or outside work. The balance of your own preferences with that of others has an implication in the decisions that you make as an individual and in a team.

25

3

Implications of style and role preferences

In the preceding two chapters you have identified some of your preferences to the way you work and the way you relate to other people.
From the descriptions of your Personal Style and your Team Role, you
will have already started to identify some areas where your preference
is a positive benefit and some areas where it can be a block to effective
working. The exercises at the end of the chapters help in starting the
process of thinking about the implications of your personal preferences
and the effects that they might have on others. In this chapter, we
investigate these implications in more depth and look at the positive
advantage of balancing our own perceptions with those of others.

Your personal style preference

Your overall style as identified in Chapter 1 has its strengths and
weaknesses, especially when applied to the world of problem solving
and decision making. The strength of your preference towards one of
the pairs makes it harder for you to appreciate and understand the
other perspective, and thus it is more difficult for you to balance your
perception.

Exercise

Take some time to reflect on what that style means in your working and non-
work environment and list the strengths and weaknesses that you can identify. You may find it useful to use a SWOT chart to help you to organise your
thoughts. SWOT stands for Strengths, Weaknesses, Opportunities and
Threats and it represents a process for analysing a particular situation.
Strengths and Weaknesses apply to the situation internally – things that you

do and that are within your own control; Opportunities and Threats are external influences on the situation – things outside your control that have an effect on the situation. For instance if you have a strong Intuitor/Perceiver preference, a strength may be your ability to come up with lots of ideas on a problem; a weakness might be the avoidance of existing solutions; an opportunity may exist in the demand for innovative solutions by the business world; a threat could be the business recession causing business to take less risk.

Fig 3.1 SWOT analysis of personal style preference

STRENGTHS	WEAKNESSES
OPPORTUNITIES	THREATS

Now ask yourself the following questions. They will help you gain a further insight into your personal style and its implications for your own effectiveness:

- How does my personal style enhance the work that I do?
- How does my personal style conflict with the work that I do?
- How many of my friends and colleagues have a similar style to mine?
- How do I respond to people who have a similar style?
- How many of my friends and colleagues have a different style to mine?
- How do I respond to people who have a different style?
- What benefits could I gain by listening to people who have a different style?
- What benefits could I gain by questioning people who have a similar style?
- How would someone with the opposite style preference to mine approach the work that I do?

Refer back to Chapter 1 for some ideas and pointers on strengths and weaknesses and the preferences of different styles.

The personal style preference measured by the Myers-Briggs Type Indicator and similar instruments often helps people to identify why people are more suited to some jobs than others. The typology is often used in career counselling and interview situations to determine the best fit between the job requirements and the individual preferences. It is also useful to help people to understand why they are having problems with all or part of the job that they are being asked to perform. (The style also relates to the non-work side of the individual as well and all comments about the use of these tools in organisation life apply equally to family and social situations.)

Likes and dislikes at work

Your own personal analysis in the exercise above will show you some of the implications for your own style in your own environment. As human beings we have a built-in preference for harmony and avoidance of pain and conflict. This gives us a tendency to move towards the parts of our work that we enjoy – that is the parts of our work where our style preference is in tune with the job demands, and to move away or avoid those parts of our work that we do not enjoy – the parts where the demands are in conflict with our style preference.

Exercise

Ask yourself the following questions about the work that you do. (If you do not have a job, or wish to extend the analysis, ask the questions about a non-work situation.)

- What parts of your job do you enjoy doing?
- What parts of your job do you not like doing?
- Do you tend to favour the parts of your job that you enjoy and put them high on your priority list?
- Do you tend to avoid the parts of your job that you do not enjoy and put them low (or miss them off) your priority list?
- What are the implications for creating this imbalance in your job?

David Keirsey and Marilyn Bates have simplified the complexity of the full Myers-Briggs Type Indicator analysis by suggesting four 'temperaments' that have an overriding effect on our actions.[1] The four temperaments are identified by two of the four preferences: SP, SJ, NT and NF. Looking at Keirsey and Bates' analysis of these temperaments, one can identify those parts of work that are liked and disliked by each temperament.

[1] David Kiersey and Marilyn Bates, *Please Understand Me*, Prometheus Nemesis Books, 1978

Table 3.1

LIKES AND DISLIKES AT WORK

	Likes	Dislikes
SP	Trouble shooting. Emergencies and pressure. Dealing with practical problems. Variety. Being busy.	Inactivity. Monotony Areas with lack of freedom. Situations with little or no clear information. Being idle.
SJ	Meeting deadlines. Working to established structures and procedures. Attention to detail. Planning and organising.	Unclear objectives. Changes of plan. Ambiguity. Lack of control.
NT	Opportunity to question systems. Producing ideas. Freedom to act. Recognition by peers.	Routine. Detail. Bureaucratic procedures. Dealing with relationships.
NF	'People centred' activities. Helping others. Doing things for others. Turning problems into opportunities. Supportive cultures.	Situations that have a potential for disagreement or conflict. Refusing requests for help. Criticism. Dealing with people who are depressed.

29

Looking at the list of likes and dislikes in Table 3.1, may trigger some more ideas about the way you tend to favour some parts of your job more than others in your analysis of the implications of personal style on your situation.

Balance

As first discussed in Chapter 1, a more effective perception of a problem or situation can be made when your own personal preference is counterbalanced by a different or opposing viewpoint. The strength of your own likes and perceptions is then enhanced by the different position.

The easiest way to the different viewpoint is to ask someone who has a different perception for their opinion. Practising active listening to their ideas will help you to form a holistic picture of the issue and make a more balanced assessment of what to do. Active listening will also allow you to develop a greater awareness of the other viewpoint and learn to value the difference, rather than our more normal approach of dismissing differences as being wrong. When you have managed to develop this overall awareness and valuing of the alternative preference, it will be easier for you to think for yourself about the whole situation without the need to refer to another individual for the information.

Your team role preference

Much of organisation life today revolves around group work. The trend to re-engineer organisations and focus on flatter organisation structures has placed more emphasis on the team as the decision making body, not the individual manager. Studies of teams over recent years, especially in the quality field, have confirmed the theory that they are often better placed to make decisions, and therefore make a better decision. We can expect a further growth in the importance of team work and team problem solving as these trends continue to move into organisations that have had a more traditional approach. Understanding and working effectively with our own personal preference for working in a team situation is therefore growing in importance.

In Chapter 2 you identified your own role preference. If you have completed the inventory in Appendix 1, you will also have identified the strength of that preference and your immediate back-up and alternative roles. Consider the strengths and weaknesses of your role in the job that you perform. (Remember that the role preference dictates how you approach working in a group or team situation, when working individually the role will have an effect, but it will not be as clearly defined.)

Fig 3.2 SWOT analysis of team role preference

STRENGTHS	WEAKNESSES
OPPORTUNITIES	THREATS

Exercise

Think about situations where you work in a group or team environment. Carry out a SWOT analysis of your own role preference.
Now ask yourself the following questions to gain a further insight into your role and its implications for your own effectiveness:

- How does my role preference assist the teams that I am a member of?
- How does my role preference hinder the teams that I am a member of?
- How many of my team colleagues have a similar role to mine?
- How do I respond to people who have a similar role?
- How many of my team colleagues have a different role to mine?
- How do I respond to people who have a different role?
- What benefits could I gain by listening to people who have a different style?
- What benefits could my teams gain by balancing the roles in the team?

31

Refer back to Chapter 1 for some ideas and pointers on strengths and weaknesses and the preferences of different roles.

The best results come from teams where there is a balance of the team roles. This was one of the findings of the research carried out by Professor Belbin at Henley.[2] It is therefore important that we all understand the value to the team of each of the roles and learn to build on the differences rather than dismiss them. The person with the different role in the team has very often become the butt of criticism and denigration, the scapegoat for problems. When conducting team building sessions using the team role analysis, several individuals have been amazed and relieved to discover that their own personal preferences were not only OK but were a positive benefit to the team. The other team members have also been suitably astonished that the 'mis-fit' was in fact a valuable member of the team. Resulting from these discoveries not only are relationships more harmonious, but also results improve.

[2] R. Meredith Belbin, *Management Teams – Why They Succeed or Fail*, Heinemann, 1981

Preferences when not in a team

Although the research on team roles was conducted on how people worked in groups, there are some obvious implications for people at an individual level in how their team role preference affects their approach to situations. It is fairly clear that someone with a creative preference in a team would also tend to come up with ideas when working on individual projects. If they were a Creator, then their approach would tend to be one of coming up with ideas and not following them through to implementation. Whilst this tendency can be balanced in a team, it is not so easy to compensate for this bias when working on your own.

The individual roles have their implications in how we approach situations, some combinations of role (where someone has two or more roles in close preference) also have implications. For instance, the combination of Creator/Driver is a dangerous one in a leader or manager. This person has the ability to come up with ideas, and the power and drive to push them through against opposition. In a conversation with one of the most senior officers in the Royal Navy, he recognised this problem in himself. His profile was strongly Creator/Driver. On doing the analysis with me he recognised that what he had instinctively done for all of his years of command was to balance his own preferences with another viewpoint. He had always chosen as his second-in-command someone who would question his decisions and plans strongly. His last second-in-command in the service was present in the same discussion. When he carried out the team role analysis, he was a strong Evaluator. The weakness and implication of the preferred style was balanced by a different viewpoint.

Exercise

Consider how your team role affects your normal working preference:

- How does my role preference affect the way I approach situations as an individual?

- What are the implications of this approach for my work and home situation?

- Does the combination of my primary and back-up roles produce a pattern of working that reduces my potential effectiveness?

- What effect does your role preference have on your actions and approach when in a leadership or supervisory position?

As leaders we will exhibit the same tendencies and prejudices as a team member. But, as the leader we set the climate and 'the way we do things round here', all of which will be affected by our own preference. Our team role can therefore have an unbalancing effect on the team and those who work for us. They may be tempted to play down their own role and try to comply with the behaviour pattern of the leader in order to please. As the analysis of effective team and group work has shown, rather than improve the situation, this tendencies will make matters worse. Individuals need to be given the confidence to express alternative views and perceptions without fear of reprisal. That again suggests that we should put a great deal of effort into ensuring that people are both aware of their own preferences and also value the differences. As leaders, it is our responsibility to set an example and to 'walk the talk'.

Team roles and redundancy

Recent surveys of managers who have been made redundant have highlighted further implications for people with particularly strong team role preferences.[3] They have found that the people being discarded by their companies were showing a higher proportion of Drivers, Creators and Investigators than the other roles. In times of trouble, one might have expected that these would be the roles in demand, but it appears that as far as their employers are concerned, the strengths of their role were more than compensated for by their weaknesses. The reports highlight cases where forthrightness is displayed at the expense of shrewdness; imagination with no regard for realism of the situation at hand. When times are hard and the knives are out, the victims appeared to have been those individuals who were well equipped for executive work in their role strengths, but were bereft of the political ability to survive in organisational life.

If Drivers, Creators and Investigators were the most likely roles to be discarded, the roles that displayed the most resilience in the recessionary cut-backs were Implementers, Finishers, Evaluators and Co-ordinators. The common theme to all of these roles is that they are objective oriented, and appear to have a greater grasp of the situational reality. They may not have the spark of dynamism or creativity, but they are also less likely to rock the boat.

33

[3] Research by Cranfield Business School, Pauline Hyde and Associates, University of Manchester and Coutts Career Consultants quoted in 'At last: an impartial gauge of deep recession' by Michael Dixon, *Financial Times*, 13 March 1992

Table 3.2

TEAM ROLES AND LEADERSHIP

Team role	Implications as a Leader
Coordinator	Can employ her or his talents overtly, remembering that effective team performance is the objective. Should be prepared to shift between taking a leading role and a team role according to the situation.
Driver	Best when operating in a team of peers. Self-discipline is required to avoid the tendency to ride roughshod over the other team members.
Creator	Must exercise considerable self-discipline and be prepared to listen to comments on proposals and ideas. Controlling a team can stifle creative output, so Creators must always keep their role objective in mind.
Evaluator	Take care not to over-dominate the other members of the team with highly developed thinking ability and be over-critical of other roles.
Implementer	Strength in clarifying objectives in practical terms, and introducing and maintaining structure in a team. Weakness in favouring action without proper planning.
Investigator	A tendency to use their power of position to concentrate too much on the development of external contacts at the expense of team work and task completion.
Communicator	Should interpret her or his role as that of a developer of others and delegator, and can carry this out overtly.
Finisher	Should be careful not to to overly control team members actions, and delegate as much as possible.

34

When it came to finding jobs again once the axe had fallen, then the pattern of survival was reversed a little. The resourcefulness and networks of Investigators meant that they were not long in unemployment. The creative dynamism of Creators also made them candidates for early re-appointment. On the other hand, Completers and Evaluators were slower than average in finding new positions. Worse of all were the Drivers. Not only were Drivers quickly discarded by organisations, they also found it more difficult to find a new position. It seems that the ability to get things done, even in the face of opposition from your colleagues, is not a trait that is highly valued by organisations in times of trouble in the UK.

What are the further implications of your own role in the light of this research?

Summary

We each have a personal style preference in the way in which we approach the world and our work, and a preference for how we work in groups and teams. Each of these preferences affects our perception and the way we like to approach problem solving and decision making. It's OK to behave according to your preference, each viewpoint and role is valuable. Each preference has its strengths and weaknesses. Very often we will tend to associate with people who have similar preferences and reject those who think differently. It is useful to have the widest perspective possible when making an assessment of issues, situations and problems. A balanced perspective is more effective than a biased perspective. Self-knowledge and knowledge of others' preferences is a first step to understanding and valuing other viewpoints and approaches. Analysis of the implications of our own personal preferences can assist in developing our own organisational future and survival.

35

4

What sort of problem am I facing?

There is a long-standing debate, sometimes heated argument, between the rational manager and the creative manager that can never be resolved so long as the two camps persist in trench warfare. Each side makes claims to be the one right way, and is at pains to decry the other's approach. What each side rarely sees is that there is a place for both approaches and that both are right.

As we have seen in the previous chapters, we each have a preference for working in a particular way and we have a preferred way of approaching a problem and making a decision. We have also seen that each preferred approach or style has its benefits and its disadvantages, its strengths and its weaknesses. My proposal is that a more balanced approach can be more effective in dealing with the complexities of the modern world, and give higher quality solutions and decisions. This includes balancing the creative and analytical approaches and using the most appropriate style for the situation.

But surely a balanced approach takes time, and that is one commodity that we are painfully short of in today's rapidly changing environment. The amount of time spent in soliciting other viewpoints, looking for alternative ideas and checking your perception cannot be justified. There is no time to think or to delay, we must solve problems quickly and get on with implementing decisions. 'He who hesitates is lost' is a familiar cry, whether it is a logical analyser or a creative entrepreneur who is the mouthpiece.

As you are spending time reading this book and have not yet consigned it to the bookshelf or returned it to the library, I can assume that you are reading with a fairly open mind, and willing to consider some new information and ideas. So take a few minutes now to think about the decisions that you have made in the last few days, and the problems that you faced. Write them down and put them into some form of priority order of importance or significance.

How long did you spend on these problems in the stages of collecting information, analysing that information and making a decision?

How many decisions were based on little or no information or data, but were based on opinion or prejudice?

What would have been the outcome if you had delayed the decision for a little time?

Thinking before acting

It is a rare decision indeed that cannot be delayed, even for a few seconds, in order to give time to think and plan. One of my early managers in Esso Petroleum taught me this when I was learning to be a supervisor. Being in charge of a distribution plant worth several million pounds and housing a volatile and dangerous product like petrol is an awesome responsibility for someone who had no technical training or experience. In my times of panic I would turn to Dennis for guidance. Dennis never gave you an unconsidered response. Even when there was a derailment of a train of fuel inside the plant, he did not give an immediate answer or directive. He always thought first, even if it was for only a few seconds. For the terror-stricken young supervisor awaiting instructions and assistance who was left holding a silent telephone for what seemed like an eternity, the words 'Thinking, lad, thinking' still remain in my memory as a reminder to think before acting. Sharing this story with other colleagues in the company I found that they too had learned the same lesson from the same mentor. Thank you, Dennis.

37

Most of us recognise the folly of jumping to a conclusion or a decision without having the right information available, yet we all do it. A favourite exercise in decision making in supervisor training courses (liked equally by trainers and participants) is to simulate a series of probable requests that are made of a supervisor each day, and get them to decide and debate their actions.

We compile most situations around company policies and people management situations, as these often have the greatest implications if an incorrect route is taken. Despite often realising that there are dire consequences for the organisation, if not for the individual, of an incorrect response, most supervisors will attempt an answer and would take action without any knowledge of the correct procedure or policy. They convince themselves that it is important to make the decision, especially if it is being asked of them by a senior manager or an outside body, like a customer. In the training room we have seen potential cases of sex and race discrimination, breaches of health and safety law, infringements of personal rights and numerous breaches of tax and employment law. All of these were avoidable if the supervisor referred to the appropriate policy manual and procedure that was available. In these cases a little knowledge and an assumption can be fatal.

Therefore in some situations it is important to recognise that there are established procedures that have been laid down to prevent the unfortunate decision maker unwittingly breaking the law, ethics or accepted standards. Creativity is not appropriate in such situations.

The need for creative and innovative thinking

Not every situation can be reduced to a series of procedural steps. The Ford Motor Company attempted to standardise their management practice in this way through a series of manuals and procedural guidelines in the hope of limiting the risk associated with delegating authority. The process worked for a number of years, but the strain of keeping the processes up to date, and the speed at which they became inappropriate made the process a millstone. Ford now train their managers to analyse situations for themselves and have delegated much of the decision making to self-managed work teams. The avoidance of risk is a common feature of the decision-making processes of the major corporations.

In opposition to the rational and rigid decision making processes, the creativity movement took up an opposing standpoint. Without taking risk there was no opportunity to innovate, and without innovation businesses stagnate. The gurus like John Adair, Edward de Bono, Tom Peters and Roger van Oech express the issue in stark, life and death terms in an attempt to make organisations and individuals break out of their internal and backward-looking focus. The chief executive of a hotel chain[1] expressed the weakness of the analytical approach like this: 'Managing a service business through internal reports is like playing tennis by keeping your eyes on the scoreboard.'

The rate of pace of change in today's world is so fast that the data collected by most businesses is totally irrelevant for decision making. To predict future growth through historic accounting is like walking backwards into the future.

[1] Isadore Sharp, CEO Four Seasons Hotels

Fig. 4.1 Comparison of accuracy of information gathered for the same time lapse and different rates of change

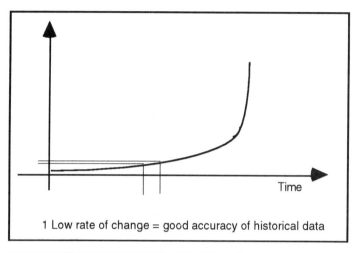

1 Low rate of change = good accuracy of historical data

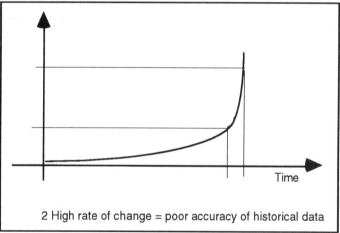

2 High rate of change = poor accuracy of historical data

The two graphs in Figure 4.1 above demonstrate graphically the danger of using historical data and old methods and procedures. When the rate of pace of change was not great, say in the 1950s, the difference in the environment between one year and the next was not significant. Policies, rules, procedures and decision making processes did not need to be changed with any regularity. The data collected on a situation was valid for some time. There was no need for innovation or creativity.

Compare that with the second graph which is more like the environment of rapid technological, political, social and economic change that we are experiencing in the 1990s. Here, the same time gap gives data that is highly inaccurate. In this situation there is a need to look forward and be creative in order to survive. There may still be time to think, but the thinking process is different.

When to be analytical, when to be creative

Some years ago Reg Revans made the distinction between a puzzle and a problem – the solution to a puzzle exists and can be found, a problem is so difficult or complex that the solution does not exist, and may never be found. David Casey developed the distinction for the business world into simple puzzles, complex puzzles and problems.[2]

Casey isolates simple puzzles as being those technical issues that can be managed within a single function or by an individual. They are often situations where there is a right answer, such as calculations, carrying out routine work, solving crossword puzzles. More complex problems involve the co-operation of others and a process or system to reach a solution. The answer does exist, but it takes a little more effort to find it. Examples might be bringing a new product from design to the marketplace, introducing a new computer system, finding a new job, putting together a corporate operating plan.

Problems exist at the highest level where there is no known, or right answer. Developing a vision and long term plan for the organisation, deciding on an individual career path, responding to new social trends, finding a solution to long-term unemployment. As one moves from the simple puzzle to the problem the level of uncertainty increases, as does the need for co-operation and creativity. That is not to say that creativity and innovation has no place at lower levels of problem solving, but that at the higher levels, the rational and analytical approach is less relevant, and is often dangerous. Figure 4.2 shows the barrier that exists between the methods appropriate for solving puzzles and the methods appropriate for solving problems.[2]

Creativity has its place in puzzle solving, especially in creating new ways of working. The continuous improvement movement of Total Quality Management utilises an innovative problem-solving process to question the status quo and find improved ways of working. No process or procedure is above the scrutiny of the improvement teams and

[2] David Casey, 'When is a team not a team', *Personal Management*, January 1985

Fig. 4.2 Problems and puzzles

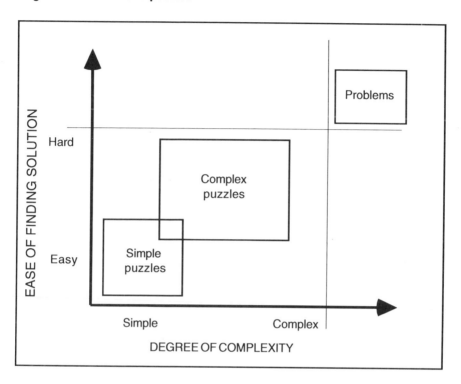

quality circles in their quest to rid the organisation of out-dated practices and bureaucracy. However, some organisations have found that they have so many improvements and changes taking place that the organisation is in a state of turmoil and little physical work gets done. Innovation can be overdone, what may be needed is a balance between looking for improvements and realising the benefits from the improvement before changing the practice again.

When to use a particular approach depends on the situation and the circumstances. What must be recognised is that there are different styles, and no one is the right way, all of the time. When the problem is a puzzle, then an analytical approach is more relevant, when the problem is a problem, then an analytical approach is not appropriate. Creative and innovative approaches are necessary to deal with problems, and they can be useful in creating improved ways of working on puzzles, though their overuse can be destructive.

(To avoid confusion in the rest of the book, the distinction between puzzle and problem is assumed and is not highlighted by the use of the different terms. The generic term 'problem' is used throughout to describe the situation or issue that needs to be addressed and progressed towards the development of a solution or strategy for action.)

Creative and rational approaches

The best known of the problem analysis techniques in common use was developed by Charles Kepner and Benjamin Tregoe in the 1960s. The Kepner-Tregoe approach introduces a systematic approach to the logical and rational process of analysing a problem so that a cause is located on which corrective action is taken. It seeks to set up a series of questions and specifications to help the collection of data and its analysis. Following the process, managers find that the solutions almost jump out at them once the problem has been correctly analysed. Clear progression from one step to the next prevents the manager from making irrational jumps of logic or unsystematic thinking.

By contrast with the systematic approaches, the creative approaches often make a point of their unconventional nature. Lateral thinking, brainstorming and other similar techniques deliberately break the 'straight line thinking' and favour the random association of ideas in a process that breaks away from reduction analysis. Taking leaps into the fantasy world and allowing free expression, a number of interesting possibilities are then tested for their feasibility and refined into a workable solution.

Neither can be identified as better than the other. Major breakthroughs and important discoveries and solutions have come from both approaches. The discovery of the structure of the DNA molecule was the result of painstaking, rational analysis. The active suspension on racing cars was the result of a lateral thinking exercise. What we can do is be aware of our own preference for one approach or the other and to be more aware of the possibility of taking an alternative way.

The Western education system tends to favour the rational approach to thinking and problem solving at the expense of the creative and intuitive. Our school learning is still based on determining causes, showing reasoning, detailed analysis, and learning procedures and rules. Some freer expression is being developed, but the examination and testing system that dominates the education world automatically skews teaching to those things that can be tested easily.

In the personal style analysis in Chapter 1, we noticed a population distribution that favoured the Senser over the Intuitor by a factor of three to one. The other predominantly creative style is the Perceiver, where there is an equal split with the Judging tendency. The combination of NP (Intuitor/Perceiver) is found in only 12 per cent of the population. The research carried out by Meredith Belbin showed that the Creator was the second lowest preferred team role for executives after Finisher. The creative approach therefore has the odds stacked against it, which probably accounts for the numerous books that have been written on the need for innovation and creativity, and the relatively few books that exist on the rational decision-making process.

The aim in this book is to present a situational approach and to acknowledge and value the alternative approaches. Sometimes the rational is appropriate and effective, sometimes the creative is appropriate and effective. There is no one right way, but there is a process that allows us to combine the two approaches and ensure that whichever is used, we achieve the best result.

Summary   43

There is always time to think before you act. Even in the most extreme cases, a few milliseconds of thought can help. The thinking time can help you to decide whether the situation that you are facing requires a creative or an analytical approach. These are just two different ways of problem solving, neither is right or wrong, and neither has universal application. There is a need for balance between the two in order to use the most appropriate approach in each situation. The environment is making changes at such a rate that we need to collect as much information as possible from as many sources in order to make effective decisions.

5

Ready – Aim – Fire

Given all of the differences there are between people, all of our different approaches to problem solving, and all of the different types of problems that we face, is there one right way to approach a problem that guarantees success?

With all of the potential differences, there is no one right way, but there is an approach that ensures more effective decision making and takes a balanced approach rather than relying too heavily on one set of perceptions or on one preference for a particular approach. That balanced approach is Ready – Aim – Fire.

Ready – Aim – Fire

The idea of Ready – Aim – Fire derives from the military approach to firing a gun. Before pulling the trigger (Fire) you want to make sure that you know what it is that you are going to shoot at and that you have the appropriate weapon (Ready). It is not very effective in warfare to shoot at high-altitude aircraft with a rifle, and it is also not very effective to use a missile on rifle range. The Ready stage of the weapons procedure makes sure that you have all of the possible information available on the target and the options available to you before moving on to the next stage – Aim.

Aiming involves selecting the right weapon for the job, focusing on the target, and taking aim. The element of chance is reduced by the selection process and the ability for the individual or the battery commander to now eliminate all other options and possibilities, close the mind to all distractions and focus on the target. Only when the first two stages of Ready – Aim have been correctly completed is the order given to go into action – Fire.

If one of these steps is missed out or not competed properly then mistakes are made and chaos often ensues. In the dangerous arena of warfare these mistakes often have catastrophic consequences. Innocent people get injured because the target is not properly identified – even to the extent that in warfare you kill people on your own side as is graphically illustrated in conflicts like the Gulf War. Diplomatic incidents are created by individuals taking action before considering the options and consequences. Whole armies and countries have been drawn into conflicts due to the headstrong action of one or two individuals. Indiscriminate firing inflicts horrific casualties among civilian populations for no strategic advantage.

When operating in a UN peacekeeping role, a single transgression from the rules of engagement by the 'blue berets' can escalate the tension beyond their capacity for containment. Examples appear on our television screens daily. It is no wonder that military training programmes put so much emphasis on following the right procedures and the terms of reference for their involvement.

Ready – Aim – Fire in problem solving 45

I do not want to suggest that all organisations should be run on military lines, though there are a number of parallels and lessons that can be applied. But we can take their Ready – Aim – Fire approach that limit mistakes in weapons deployment and apply it to problem solving and decision making in an organisation environment and thereby limit mistakes in our decision making. We can use it to make more effective decisions. So how does Ready – Aim – Fire work in problem solving?

First complete the Ready stage: identify the target, that is identify the problem that needs to be solved or the decision that needs to be made. This means gathering all the information that you need to identify the scope of the problem, defining its limits and collecting ideas on options available. Once this stage is complete, then move onto the Aiming stage.

Choose the best solution or strategy from the information that you have amassed in the previous stage. (Very often by defining the problem and thinking about what is needed, the solution becomes much easier to identify.)

Once the solution or strategy is identified, then go into action – Fire.

It is a simple process – one that ensures that you gather all of the information that you need before you make a decision and go into action. However, it is process that most of us find difficult to follow in practice, either individually or when we are involved in group work or in organisations. That is because of our own personal preference for

Fig. 5.1 Ready – Aim – Fire

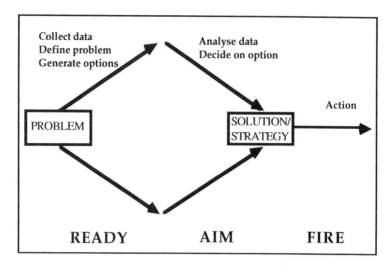

working in a particular way that favours one or other of the three steps. We may like collecting data and developing options and therefore never get out of the Ready stage. We may favour analysis and get so paralysed by the process that we take no action. Or we may favour action and jump too readily to conclusions. Whatever our preference, we are unlikely to follow the balanced approach of Ready – Aim – Fire, unless we understand the benefits and take some positive action to learn to include the other steps.

The case of Marcia's Chip Shop

Marcia is the daughter of a successful fish and chip shop owner in a small town in the north-east of Scotland. After she had taken her finance and accountancy examinations at college, her father decided that the time was right to open another fish and chip shop in the town and give Marcia the opportunity to join and expand the family business.

The business was successful. The combination of fresh fish, fresh potatoes hand cut into chips, best quality oils and a family recipe batter produced from the best quality ingredients and mixed daily, made sure that the quality of the product was as good as it could be. This, combined with an excellent personal service meant that people travelled from far outside the immediate catchment area to buy their fish and chips at the shop. There were competitive shops in the town, but they often cut corners and quality by using frozen fish, pre-cut potatoes and proprietary brands of batter mix, or by cutting back on the service so that long queues formed in the shops. Marcia's father had the strategy for success in the fish and chip business.

So he decided that the time had come to open another shop in a different part of the town to serve his customers who came from that area, and to take a larger share of the town's trade. With his daughter having been brought up in the traditions and best practices of the existing shop, and now having obtained the academic background to oversee a business enterprise, the time was right.

Premises were purchased in the chosen area, equipment bought and installed and all of the experience of running a successful business in the town was put to use. The final decision that had to be made was on the packaging for the fish and chips. There was to be no compromise on the quality or style of the ingredients – no frozen fish or pre-cut chips, but there was a question about how you presented and wrapped them.

Up to now the choice had been a traditional one – greaseproof paper, brown paper and newspaper. First of all the fish and chips would be wrapped in grease proofpaper, then in a sheet of brown paper to seal the oils and stop leakage, then wrapped in old newspaper to keep the heat from escaping. The style was effective, it had customer approval and it was cost efficient. However, there were alternatives available and a trial set up to evaluate the options.

A test fry of fish and chips was divided between the different packaging options. There were polystyrene trays for the fish and chips to sit in before being wrapped that replaced the greaseproof paper bags. Foil containers like those used by the Chinese take-away trade were included in the test. Hamburger style polystyrene boxes provided insulation and protection from the leakage of oils and sauces in one unit. Different wrappings were tried to replace the newspaper. In all, about six different packaging combinations were tested alongside their existing traditional approach.

Once the fish and chips had been loaded into the different containers, they were put into a car and driven around the area for about ten minutes. This was to recreate the conditions that most customers would experience – they come out from their home to buy the fish and chips for the family supper, put them on the floor of the car (passenger side) with the heater on to keep food as warm as possible, then driving home to serve the meal to the family. (Despite the common image of fish and chips being eaten out of the wrapping as you walk long the street, the reality of the TV dinner and the age of the motor car means that most portions are now taken home to eat.)

Marcia's father was at pains to create the exact environment for the test – he wanted to simulate real life as much as possible so that they could evaluate the results in the knowledge that they were making a decision on the best information available.

The crucial time came when the packages were opened, one by one, and the contents sampled. The different packages were compared on a number of important customer criteria: their ability to retain heat in the food between the shop and the home; the ability to maintain the crispness of the food; the ability to protect the car and clothing from leakage of oils and sauces; the ease of opening and serving. When all of these different criteria had been evaluated, the packaging that won the day was the old-fashioned greaseproof paper, brown paper and newspaper method that they had been using for years. When they then came to comparing the price, it was also the cheapest available option.

Marcia's father had taken methodical steps to follow a Ready – Aim – Fire approach to making the decision on packaging. His own instinct told him that the old way was the best, but he had no proof, no basis on which to make that assertion that they should keep on with the same system. As customer service not cost was the guiding principle of his business (he had resisted other, much greater cost-saving opportunities) he knew that the only way to decide was on the basis of a trial of the options available.

48

All possible alternatives were amassed, whether the initial reaction was one that suggested that they would not be suitable. (The foil tray was immediately thought to be inappropriate, but was included in the test.) Criteria were established on which to make the decision (Ready). A test carried out and the results evaluated to give a balanced decision (Aim) to implement when selling fish and chips to the customers at the new shop (Fire).

(As a footnote to the story, Marcia decided that she did not want to run a fish and chip shop and instead she put her financial qualifications to work in the oil industry in Aberdeen. However, the shops are still running, they are still very successful with an ever-growing reputation for quality and service, and they still wrap the fish and chips in the traditional way.)

In the above case it would have been easier for Marcia's father to have copied the successful model he already had and not to spend so much time and effort in evaluating options, especially when he didn't make a change. Why bother to look for problems where they don't exist? 'If it ain't broke – don't fix it.' Hindsight always has the ability of 20:20 vision, but luckily people like Marcia and her father understand the need to seek for continuous improvement in order to stay in touch, and hopefully ahead, of their competitors.

Many larger firms have taken the easy option of trying to replicate a previous successful formula without changes, often with devastating results. When Marks & Spencer opened their first store in Paris, they recreated their successful UK model down to the last detail. The last detail included the carrier bags then being used in the UK that sported a Union Flag design and the wording 'Buy British – Keep British Jobs'. Not the sort of advertisement to attract a French shopper away from Galeries Lafayette!

On the other hand, David Lloyd almost guarantees success with each of his new tennis centres by applying demographics. He has extensive data on his computer databases on the profile of his current membership. He uses that information to scan the public census and population information databases to identify areas that have a concentration of people with similar demographic profile (Ready). Armed with that information and the choices available, he can focus his attention on the best potential areas and development sites available in order to make an investment decision (Aim). The carrying out of the implementation plan (Fire) is then a simple process of building the centre and taking the fees off the waiting players and teams.

Ready – Aim – Fire and personal style preference

In Chapter 1 you identified your own personal style preference and looked at some of the implications of that style in relation to the way you perceived things, the way you analysed information and the way you preferred to take decisions. There are obvious connections between the personal style preferences that you noted there and your position on the Ready – Aim – Fire process.

Those with a Perceiving preference will enjoy the Ready stage – they are interested in creating options and resisting closure; those with a Judging preference will want to skip over the Ready – Aim stages to get into action as quickly as possible.

The Ready stage is one that is also an opportunity for creativity and innovation, so it is more favoured by Intuitors. Sensors will enjoy collecting the data and historical analysis of the problem associated with the Ready stage, but they are impatient with theory and not as inclined towards developing possibilities and ideas, preferring to make decisions and move on.

Thinkers and Feelers focus on Aiming from their own different perspectives. It is easy for a Thinking/Introvert to find the logical analysis of a problem so fascinating that they will lock themselves away for days. Equally a Feeling/Introvert may be inclined to weigh up the possibilities and look for the perfect solution. For them the Aiming is the answer, and you may never need go into action.

Our own style preference will lead us to prefer part of the Ready – Aim – Fire approach. Our strength of preference in the style will lead us to different levels of preference – sometimes to the complete exclusion and devaluing of a complete step or two.

Exercise

Refer to your personal style preference identified in Chapter 1 and take some time to reflect on the following questions that relate to those styles and your own profile.

- How does that style tend to favour one or two parts of the Ready – Aim – Fire process?
- How does your own preference for each part of the Ready – Aim – Fire process match up with the style tendencies?
- Which stage of the Ready – Aim – Fire process do you favour most?
- What are the implications for you in the different roles that you may have? At work? At home? In a social environment? In voluntary work? On committees? In learning?
- What examples of problems can you find from work and from other situations?
- What would have been the possible outcome by following a balanced Ready – Aim – Fire approach?
- Who, among your colleagues and friends, can you identify who has a different preference for their problem solving approach?
- What opportunities can you foresee to balance your preferences with others to create a Ready – Aim – Fire approach?

Ready – Aim – Fire and team roles

Just as our personal style preference can affect our problem-solving approach, so the team role will also have a guiding effect on which part of the process we tend to favour.

Ready

There are three roles aligned with the Ready stage: Creator, Investigator and Communicator. Creators like ideas generation and creativity.

Table 5.1

POSSIBLE PREFERENCES TO READY-AIM-FIRE FOR EACH OF THE SIXTEEN TYPES

ISTJ	ISFJ	INFJ	INTJ
Aim-Fire	Aim-Fire	Ready-Fire	Ready-Fire
ISTP	ISFP	INFP	INTP
Ready-Aim	Ready-Aim	Ready-Aim	Ready-Aim
ESTP	ESFP	ENFP	ENTP
Ready-Aim	Ready-Aim	Ready-Aim	Ready-Aim
ESTJ	ESFJ	ENFJ	ENTJ
Aim-Fire	Aim-Fire	Ready-Fire	Ready-Fire

Table 5.2

PREFERENCES TO READY-AIM-FIRE FOR EACH OF THE TEAM ROLES

READY	CREATOR INVESTIGATOR COMMUNICATOR
AIM	EVALUATOR FINISHER (part role)
FIRE	DRIVER COORDINATOR IMPLEMENTER FINISHER (part role)

They are interested in developing new concepts and options. Investigators do not have the primary creativity of the Creator, the inputs are not new ideas, but are options and information on which to make decisions. Communicators work creative thoughts and data collection around relationships.

All three roles are more concerned with the ideas and the data than they are with the implementation of any of them. People who are strong in these roles find them difficult to follow any routine, are bored with carrying out projects and often find it difficult to make decisions between options. They much prefer to allow others to make the decision and carry out the plan while they carry on developing options and amassing data. (But if you want a novel or innovative way of making a decision, then the Creator or Investigator will give you some ideas on the process!)

Aim

The analytical process of Aim is only favoured by two of the team roles, and in the case of the Finisher, that is only a part role. The Evaluator role carries the primary responsibility for weighing up the data and options and asking the 'what if' questions that allow for the correct decisions to be made. The Finisher role is concerned with time constraints and completion of tasks, and part of that energy is directed to making sure that the strategy or decision is feasible – that there is enough time and other resources to complete the task. The other part of the role energy is directed into completing and finishing actions – actually doing the task rather than deciding what to do.

Once again, individuals who have a strong preference for one of the Aiming roles will value that function more than any other. They are not concerned with idea generation or options. In fact they often see new ideas as being irrelevant to the process of making a correct decision.

Fire

The majority of the roles in the team role analysis are action roles. They are concerned with the Fire process of implementing the decision. Coordinators will draw action together on an objective basis to keep focused on the outcome. Drivers will use their energy to shape the decision into action and galvanise people into action. Implementers will draw up schedules and action plans to ensure that the task is well organised. Finally, as we have already seen, Finishers will use part of their energy to complete a task.

Teams

As we have discussed in earlier analysis, people will find that their approach to problems is guided by their role preference. Whilst that causes an imbalanced decision making process as an individual, when we group together in teams or organisations, the combination of role preferences causes even greater imbalances to take place.

Fig. 5.2 Ready – Aim – Fire and team roles

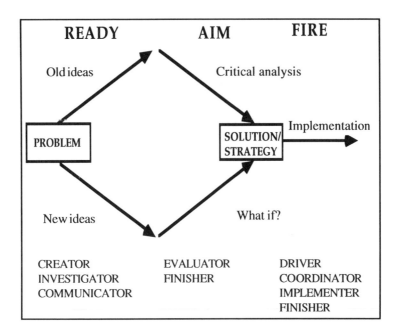

Just look at Table 5.2 again. If we create a team that will achieve the best result, then Belbin's research and analysis would create that team with someone in each of the eight roles who has a strong preference for that role. That means there will be a natural bias to Ready – Fire and a further bias to Fire, based purely on the numerical strength of the preference to Ready – Aim – Fire in the team. If, however, we believe that each of the parts of the Ready – Aim – Fire sequence is as important as the other, then the three-and-a-half roles in Fire need to value and respect the one and a half Aim roles and give them equal air time and importance in the decision making process.

Equally, the three Ready roles need to have a similar respect for Evaluators and Finishers, who are their usual adversaries – ideas people are not usually great friends with those whose propensity is to shoot down their suggestions. Yet for the decision making and problem solving process to work in an effective and balanced way, they must find a way of working as equal partners.

So, even a balanced Belbin team is not automatically an effective problem solving unit. The essential addition action to make the team work effectively is that each member of the team must value each other's role and not play their own role to an extreme where it becomes dysfunctional. That means each team member understanding their own role and the importance of that role in the team performance; understanding everyone else's role and their value and place in the team performance; how the roles work together and balance each other; and how they relate to the problem-solving process.

Very few teams in existence will be balanced in the team roles. Because they will have been assembled on other criteria, the team roles will be mixed and there will be a bias towards one of the stages of the Ready – Aim – Fire process. These teams will have an even greater problem to follow a balanced decision making process, and will be less effective.

Exercise

Refer to your team role identified in Chapter 2 and take some time to reflect on the following questions.

- How does your role affect your approach to problem solving and decision making?

- How does your experience match up with the tendencies in Table 5.2?

- Does your preference for a stage of the Ready – Aim – Fire process in the team role analysis match the preference in your personal style analysis?

- When you are working in groups and teams, do you find that you are working with people who have a similar preference or a different preference?

- What is your reaction to those who have a similar preference?

- What is your reaction to those who have a different preference?

- Can you identify people who fill each of the three stages of the Ready – Aim – Fire process? What would be the effect of these people working together on a project?

- Can you identify imbalanced teams from your own experience? How have their results been affected by this imbalance?

- Can you identify balanced teams from your own experience? Have their results been significantly different from imbalanced teams?

- Identify your current teams – at work – in other situations? What are the team roles of the members? What is the balance of the team? How does that balance affect the team decision making? Who is the leader of the team? How does her/his preference affect the team decision making approach?

Team leadership

Team leaders have an effect on the working of the team as we discussed in Chapter 3. With the added bias towards one of the problem solving stages, the team can be led into inappropriate action by its leader pressing her or his own preferred approach.

One could envisage that the most effective Belbin team would be one that had a balance of all of the roles where each person understood and valued the other's role, but also operated on a self-managed basis. Leadership would be shared in the team and the leader at any particular moment would be the person most appropriate for the stage of the problem solving process.

Thus, a Creator and/or Investigator might take the lead in the Ready stage. An Evaluator would lead the team to a decision in Aiming with a Finisher checking that the decision is feasible given the resource constraints. To get into action, the leadership would be shared between the Driver and the Coordinator who would keep the team focused on the outcome and objective with sufficient drive and enthusiasm to complete the task. At the same time the Implementer would schedule the work and lead the team in getting the task complete, and the Finisher leader would ensure that all of the loose ends were tied up and the project completed on schedule and on budget. Finally, should any conflict occur throughout the project, the Communicator would take the lead in developing a solution and recreating harmonious working relationships.

55

A flight of fancy, perhaps. Though my experience is that where these ideas of the team balance and the problem solving sequence have been put across in a work situation, even imbalanced teams have come to recognise the practical benefits behind the approach and have adopted such a pattern of working. No longer is the most senior person the leader of the team. More often the leadership choice is made on the ability of the individual to co-ordinate a project or on the basis of their suitability for the stage of the process. Leadership need not be fixed, it can be a flexible activity shared by the whole team. Teams then find that they become more effective.

Organisation imbalance

Individuals are imbalanced in the problem solving process due to their personal style preference and the effect of their team role on their actions. Teams are imbalanced due either to the imbalance of the team roles between the problem solving stages, or due to an imbalance of the team roles in the team. What about organisations (which often operate as large teams). What happens to organisations when there is an imbalance of the Ready – Aim – Fire process? Why would an organisation become imbalanced in the first place?

To answer the second question first, we only need to look at how people join and are recruited by organisations. We are attracted to people that work like us and think like us. As we have seen in the first chapters, it is very easy to understand our way of working and our preferences, and ignore the benefits of other perceptions and styles. It is hard work to listen to a different point of view and to understand a different thinking process. We like people to be like us, it is much easier to understand them.

The same applies for organisations. After all, organisations are only collections of people. There is active discrimination in recruitment in favour of 'people who can fit in easily'. In other words, people who think and act like the rest of the organisation. Each organisation has its own culture – 'the way we work round here'. Even if someone slips through the initial screening net they soon find the atmosphere and way of working not to their liking and leave.

Thus the organisation recruits in its own image, or the image of one or two of its more prominent opinion leaders or successes, and gets out of balance.

Sometimes this is a positive benefit. For instance, if you were a creative agency that is famous for its radical ideas and solutions, then you would want to continue to recruit Creators and Investigators. Similarly, if you were a construction contractor, then you would want Implementers and Finishers – people who got on with the job and planned the execution and finishing of each contract. If you did not have this bias, then the basis for your success is lost; you would be losing sight of the needs of your business. However, it is this natural bias that has within it the seeds of destruction for a number of organisations who follow the 'recruiting in your own image' process to extremes. There are lessons for every organisation in being aware of the imbalance and natural bias of their business and culture, and therefore planning to avoid the excesses. What I have mentioned earlier in respect of personal preferences holds true for organisational preferences too – a weakness is very often a strength that is overplayed.

In the next chapters we look at some different organisational cultures and the effects that they have on their success, using some case studies and examples to illustrate the points. The case studies are drawn from real life examples of companies and teams that we have worked with over the past few years, and from other studies of best (and worst) practice.

Summary

Ready – Aim – Fire is the balanced approach to problem solving and decision making. It allows for an analytical or a creative style depending on the situation, and its process ensures that all the relevant information is gathered before a decision is made and implemented. It takes into account personal style and role preferences and enhances our valuing of other styles and individuals.

6

The 'Ready – Ready – Ready' organisation

The creative organisation

Some organisations or departments are composed almost entirely of ideas people – Creators and Investigators; those with Intuitive or Perceiving tendencies. They spend their energy creating new ways of working and new product ideas. A 'think tank' where non-conformance and the unconventional are the norm.

As stand-alone businesses, these creative organisations usually provide a creative service: consultancy firms, research organisations, advertising agencies, inventors and gurus. They are used by other organisations to provide a creative spark, especially when under competitive pressure. Inside organisations, the Ready – Ready – Ready approach is often found in product development, marketing, design and research departments.

They are relied upon to create the difference and to come up with a solution when the need arises. By their nature they are different to the norm. Their offices (if they have them) are cluttered and untidy, often full of toys and distractions that help to provide a creative boost; their employees dress in an unconventional way, they talk a different language and they are forever wanting to make changes and try out new ideas. Their approach helps them to be creative, and is tolerated by 'straighter' business people as a necessary evil.

But their unconventional approach alienates them from other businesses and departments, so when things are going well and the need for innovation is not high on management's agenda, they are often ignored or seen as unnecessary. Research departments are closed down or merged with more 'profitable' sides of the business. Creative agencies close down and their innovation is lost.

Creativity, chaos and cost

The creative organisation is therefore one that is constantly in flux. They change rapidly in their composition and their structure. Any study of the advertising agency world will show a bewildering series of mergers and takeovers alongside new agencies being set up by small teams spinning off from major firms, and individuals moving from employment to freelance work. In all of this activity, the customer is often left in a state of confusion and the 'back room' staff are left to tidy up the mess as much as they can. As the focus and value is placed on the Ready stage only, all of the finishing and implementation importance is lost and there is little, if any, moderation of the creativity. Ideas are the most important thing, and the more outrageous the better.

The case of the promotion company

The most successful production and promotions company in the world is famed for its wonderful sales conferences and new car launches. On the walls of its senior producers are awards and letters of appreciation and commendation from their delighted clients and admiring peers. There is constant demand for their services. Budgets of millions of dollars are not uncommon, and all of the major blue chip companies use their services. They are very successful.

However, if you scratch below the surface of success you find a different story. A story of chaos, waste, misunderstandings, delays, lack of cost control, poor management and communication. Their focus is on the creative activity of putting on a show – creating the image, designing and staging the event. They do not value the activities of cost control, planning, administration or accounting. These 'behind the scenes' activities are vital for the success and profitability of business, but not to an organisation that is Ready – Ready – Ready.

Take a typical show as an example of what normally happens – the client receives some initial ideas for the show from the production team. Very often staging ideas will not have been tried out before, and many of the event ideas will be outrageous. Some of the extreme ideas will have been filtered out during the production team's deliberations on the project, but it is still left to the client to evaluate the viability of most of the suggestions. Confronted with questions about the feasibility of the proposals, the production team go into defence mode and complain bitterly about the inability of clients to see the potential of their proposal. This is classic Creator behaviour – taking offence when ideas are rejected or questioned.

Eventually, after much debate and time wasting, and several acrimonious meetings, a project is agreed and a budget set. The production team lacks precision in putting real cost and time estimates on to its ideas and does everything in its power to avoid being limited. Again it is left to the client to do most of the thinking and pushing for realism and detail – providing the Aim activity and the roles of Evaluator and Finisher.

In the run up to the show, the plans will continue to change as the production team continues to get new ideas and pursue them. There is a great deal of in-fighting and struggles for power and leadership within the production team. Communication with the client becomes spasmodic, usually prompted by the client who is getting concerned about the changes to the plans and escalating costs.

The production team at this stage will have recruited, or co-opted a producer. She or he may have been part of the team from the start if the project has been particularly large or prestigious. The producer is typically a Creator/Driver mix. If they have come from the creative side of the business it is likely that their Creator role will be ascendant. If they have come from the world of production management or stage management, then Driver will be the dominant role. Either way, there is now another conflict in the internal workings of the production team. Many of their plans and ideas will now be questioned from within the team, either by the alternative ideas of another Creator or by the desire of the Driver to control and move forward.

Even when it comes to the actual production and staging of the event, many last minute changes will be made. There will be problems with the venue that were not foreseen at the planning stage. There will be problems with some of the new presentation ideas that do not work. Equipment is not on site, the prefabricated sets will not fit the space, the crews are badly organised. Everyone is trying to do their own thing with no co-ordination or plan. The absence of an Implementer is now felt – the person who can schedule and plan who does what and when. And the production team is also beginning to miss a Communicator, as emotions and feelings start to run high.

Under stress, the team reverts to behaviour it knows best – introduce more new ideas and make more and more suggestions. Many of these are unhelpful, given the limited time to implement them. The Driver (the producer) becomes more and more directive and tactless, fostering resentment and ill feeling within the team.

Show time eventually arrives, and is almost always a success. Just like the swan, the serene performance seen on the surface of effortless gliding across the water is provided by frantic paddling by the webbed feet under the surface. So it is with the show that appears to the audience to be a seamless production, but is in effect held together by some very strained relationships and much last minute adjustment and hard work.

After the show, the production team members move on to their next projects, often working in different teams. But the effects of the imbalanced organisation are still felt. There is a sizeable administrative staff that tries to unravel the mess of tasks left to them by the production team. No clear record of activity exists, poor records of expense and purchases, incomplete crew time records, extra costs not agreed with the client … the list is endless. In order to get any invoices processed and passed by the client, a considerable amount of work has to be done, causing endless delays and disputes. Little or no assistance is provided by the production team members to this process. Most of them are already committed to new projects – their focus is elsewhere. Those that are available to assist have no interest in the minutiae of audit and accounting processes – they are waiting for the next opportunity to put their creativity to work.

So, we have an organisation that is successful – despite itself. If it were more balanced in its approach to projects and organisation, then it could cut a great deal of its waste and provide a better service to its clients. It succeeds in the main due to its size and turnover. Many smaller organisations in the promotions industry fail because they follow the same imbalanced approach but do not generate the turnover to hide their problems or do not have the status to be able to justify inflated fees to cover their inefficiencies.

In the case above, the creativity, chaos and cost of a creative organisation can be seen. Ready – Ready – Ready means that you get some brilliant ideas and new approaches, but you also get a lot of unrealistic and unworkable ideas coupled with a confused and poor implementation plan. Much of the work of the monitoring and control has to be done by the client—whether that is another internal department or the customer.

Successful creativity

But sometimes Ready – Ready – Ready organisations seem to be successful. They often find and exploit niches in the market and set trends. They shape the way we all behave as consumers, creating paradigm shifts in thinking. An idea by itself has limited value; only by applying the idea to a problem, situation or opportunity does it gain value and become an innovation. Successful creative organisations have learned to focus their creative effort towards a goal or objective and thus eliminate some of the drawbacks of the unguided ideas generators discussed above.

The case of Swatch

The Swiss watch industry had been decimated. The quartz control mechanism, ironically invented by a Swiss watch technologist, had been exploited by the Japanese watchmaking industry after the Swiss had rejected its usefulness and potential. The Swiss watch industry was reduced, almost overnight, from a country that dominated the market to a handful of specialist producers.

The radical idea of Swatch was to treat the wrist watch as a fashion accessory. The Swatch development came from a team of creative people who managed to link modern production methods with design and marketing flair, thus creating a new market. Instead of buying a watch for its functional purpose, with a purchase of no more than one or two models per person, and with long periods between purchases, the watch had now become disposable, able to follow and lead fashion trends. People bought several Swatch watches, and matched them to their mood and clothes. Model changes and designs were introduced rapidly, and the Swatch rapidly took market share, and also created a whole new market.

The Swatch designers are still in the Ready mode – they continue to come up with new ideas, follow and start trends and to create new paradigms. This is the hallmark of success for Swatch. Further developments of the concept led to the Swatch car, Swatch cameras, Swatch portable telephones. Some of the ideas and designs work, some do not. Those that do not are quickly dropped and new ideas are immediately put into production.

The paradigm shift from 'watch as a means to tell the time' to 'watch as piece of jewellery' has also meant the revival of what remained of the Swiss watch industry. It has raised the demand for expensive watches that are now a statement of fashion and taste. Any in-flight magazine carries advertisements for expensive jewellery that also tells the time.

For Swatch, Ready – Ready – Ready seems to work. Partly because of their initial success in creating a paradigm shift, and partly because their implementation has worked. They have managed to find a way of getting their ideas beyond the creative stage and into production. They also seem to have avoided some of the costly and spectacular failures that can be seen in other innovative manufacturing organisations.

Another success story can be found in the writings and lectures of Tom Peters[1] who uses a British-based creative company, Imagination, as a leading example of the creative organisation at its best. Imagination is a

[1] Tom Peters, *Liberation Management*, Excel, 1992

mix of architects, designers, computer experts, model builders, PR people, video producers, artists, photographers and other creative people who come together into a project whenever and wherever they are needed, ignoring any functional relationships. They are led by Gary Withers, who acts as a corporate butterfly, floating around the organisation providing the creative spark where necessary, but with no line authority.

The organisation at Imagination does not really exist, except in its flexibility. They recruit people who are good, often without having a specific job available at the time. People move around freely in a lateral manner picking up tasks that interest them and making a difference. Imagination is in fact just a collection of creative projects. Things get done, so perhaps there is an Aim and Fire process there, but the primary function, as the company name suggests, is to harness the imagination of the Imagineers (as they call themselves).

Losing touch with reality

63

Part of Imagination's success depends on being able to satisfy its customers. It is this relationship that manages to keep them in touch with reality. Because it is on the leading edge of acceptability and is always seeking new paradigms, the Ready – Ready – Ready organisation has a characteristic of losing touch with reality. This does not matter too much when it is a small inventor organisation where there are a flood of ideas and one or two are picked up and used. But where the organisation has found a means to get their ideas into action, and has had previous success, then a complacency and an arrogance can grow where the belief in the idea outweighs all of the voices raised in caution.

The case of the Sinclair C5

Who in Britain over the past years could forget the spectacular fortunes of Sir Clive Sinclair? He brought the pocket calculator to the UK scene, and developed one of the world's first microcomputers. He was immensely successful in developing new ideas – identifying opportunities and creating an affordable product to meet people's needs. Then came his electric car, the Sinclair C5.

The idea of producing a low-cost, environmentally friendly town vehicle has been on the drawing boards of most of the major car manufacturers and design studios for years. General Motors had tried out a design, but it could not be made to work economically. Sinclair brought the idea to production with the same tenacity and single-mindedness that created the other successful products in his quest to make technology affordable.

His C5 was called a car, but was in fact a tricycle with limited power and range. It had a very low profile, so was difficult to see in traffic. It had no reverse gear, a top speed of 15 miles an hour and needed assistance from its pedals to go up hills. It only seated one person and was open to the weather. But it was cheap, and Sinclair was convinced that he had the answer to what people wanted.

The public did not agree. The launch was up-beat, but the public did not generally have a desire for a small, underpowered and exposed vehicle. Very few were sold and stock losses caused the sale of his computer business. 'People', he said, 'are much more resistant to change than I imagined.'[2]

For Sinclair the essential step that was missing was the critical evaluation of Aim – an Evaluator could have been asking the 'what if' questions and checking the relentless pursuit of the flawed idea.

Failure does not have to be on such a large scale. Many ideas get tried out and fail without any disastrous effects. But even small-scale failures can be avoided with a strong Aim. Some of the best alliances are often formed between Creators and Evaluators. As fast as the Creator comes up with ideas, the Evaluator monitors them out for feasibility. That way the creative cycle works faster and the best solutions come to the fore quickly.

Introducing creativity

What if the organisation lacks the creativity of Ready? The lateral thinking approach pioneered by Edward de Bono[3] is a way many organisations have put the creative spark into their traditional analytical approaches. Traditional research and development operations very often fail to see innovative solutions, even when they are clearly presented – they cannot believe that a solution can be obtained by means other than analytical research. If the idea comes from someone with no scientific or industry background then the hill they have to climb to have their idea noticed is even greater. The 'not invented here' syndrome was probably invented by R & D departments. To be Ready, an organisation needs to listen to both new and old ideas, to both creative and analytical solutions.

[2] William Davis, *The Innovators*, Genesis Productions, 1987
[3] Edward de Bono, *Lateral Thinking*, Penguin Books, 1973

The case of the cigarette filter

Back in the 1960s, cigarette manufacturers were putting more and more research money into better and more powerful filters to reduce tar and nicotine content in their cigarettes. Powerful governmental and health care pressure had been highlighting the connection between cigarette smoking and health, and printing league tables of tar and nicotine content. At the same time a change in smokers' taste for a milder cigarette was growing. The need was established to produce cigarettes with a lower tar and nicotine content.

Most of the in-house research was concentrated on the filter – trying to make them more effective by increasing the size and adding more filtration elements like carbon. These had the desired effect of reducing tar and nicotine content, but also of making the cigarette difficult to draw on. This reduced the pleasure to the smoker, and the brands were not successful.

The breakthrough came from a lateral thinking suggestion from outside the filter technology research groups. Instead of increasing the size of the filter, the idea was to increase the amount of air mixture with the smoke by putting small air-intake holes around the filter. Instead of trying to block out tar and nicotine with a stronger filter, this extra air intake reduced the amounts of tar and other products per mouthful of smoke. The effect is the same – the smoker ingests less of the harsher products and gets a milder taste. But the cost of production is much lower.

65

In the case of the cigarette filter, the traditional analytical methods of R & D were failing to produce the results – there was no real creativity. Introducing a Ready phase provided the solution that the market was seeking. In a later chapter, more techniques and tools are described that help to introduce the stage of the process that is missing in the make up of the team or organisation.

There are other examples of creative companies whose success depends on developing new products and approaches. These are the success stories of organisations who seem to have a knack of getting everything together. Perhaps they have managed to move beyond the Ready – Ready – Ready state and get to Fire. Often though, it is not the design team or the creative organisation that involves itself with implementation. They use other organisations to produce the goods and distribute them, while they get on with doing what they do best – coming up with new ideas and innovations. Many other organisations have the ideas but never seem to get anything produced or implemented. They stay in a state of Ready – Ready – Ready.

Harnessing creativity

One organisation model that allows the specialism of a creative business that can also implement is found in the 'Shamrock' style organisations described by Charles Handy.[4] The shamrock is composed of three separate leaves all on a common stem. For Handy, the three leaves represent the three main parts of the new-style organisation for the 1990s:- a small core of workers who form the basis of the enterprise and give it direction; a flexible workforce and a collection of sub-contractors who implement the plans developed in the core.

The creative organisation can exist as a 'Shamrock' in its own right, or it can be in one of the three leaves, or parts of the business. Either way, the benefits of an independent, creative input is maintained, with direction and commitment being the stem that holds the three leaves together.

Summary

Through the cases in this chapter, the Ready – Ready – Ready organisation is seen to be highly creative, but has a potential for being like an unguided missile, usually bent on self-destruction through a lack of back-up, attention to detail, or loss of contact with the customer's needs or reality. For every example of failure there is one of success. For every C5 there is a Swatch or an Imagination.

The importance of creativity and innovation can be assessed by any scanning of the economic forecasters over the last 20 years. All have predicted the need for companies to be more creative, and all comment on the lack of creativity in business. The dangers of going too far towards a Ready – Ready – Ready approach can be seen in the implementation stage of ideas. Very often they bet the company on an innovation that nobody wants, or they find that their costs escalate through lack of attention to detail. But the lack of creativity in most organisations is an even greater danger. Too often individuals with creative flair are sidelined, ignored, or at best tolerated.

In order to exist in the current economic climate, and in the future, Ready – Ready – Ready organisations must make some accommodation of Aim and Fire, either within their organisation or through alliances with others, and those who lack the Ready stage need to inject some

---

[4] Charles Handy, *The Age of Unreason*, Century Hutchison, 1989

creativity and innovation. The need for balance is ever present, and that is a rare commodity in today's organisations.

As an individual, it is equally rare to have an in-built balance of Ready – Aim – Fire, so you will need to compensate for your own personal preference. In later chapters some tools and techniques are discussed that will help to develop a balance in problem solving and decision making, whether it is to put some Aim and Fire on to your Ready process or to put in some Ready, as an individual or in an organisation.

7

The 'Ready – Fire – Aim' organisation

If Ready – Ready – Ready is the creative organisation that can leave a trail of waste and disorganisation in its wake, or just have ideas that don't get implemented, then Ready – Fire – Aim is the truly innovative organisation. At least, it is when this process is working effectively.

The traditional practice of management is to subject a situation or issue to meticulous analysis. The principle seems to be that if you collect enough data, or spend sufficient time in analysis, then either the problem solves itself, or it goes away. The culture of fear that exists in hierarchies and bureaucracies mitigates against making a decision. If you do have to make a decision, then you make sure that it is a safe one — one where there is absolutely no possibility of it being a failure. For many organisations, the avoidance of risk is more important than success. Management careers have been made by avoiding decisions and minimising risk, and that role model exists for all to see.

Many of the management thinkers in the 1980s and 1990s, from Peter Drucker to Henry Mintzberg to Tom Peters, preach the gospel of experimentation to combat the excesses of the bureaucratic organisation where nothing gets done. They champion the process of Ready – Fire – Aim. They implore us to allow people in organisations to pilot their ideas, try something out and then correct the design or plan when they have learned from the initial mistakes. Allowing people to make mistakes without fear of retribution is seen to be the way to question the status quo and shake organisations into the new economic reality.

Nearly right is OK

The Ready – Fire – Aim organisation does not waste its efforts on trying to find the perfect solution. It knows that 80 per cent correct and

on time is better than 99 per cent correct and too late. These organisations spawn new models, products and services at an alarming rate.
They have also allowed the development of one of the most amazing of
all developments in the 1990s, mass customisation – the ability to produce a customised article at the cost levels of the mass production line.
They have done it by constant experimentation with products and processes.

Some charismatic leaders have been to the fore in this process,
openly and loudly breaking the mould of the 'corporate manager', growing innovators and innovation. Some managers and organisations have
learned to change to overcome extreme competition and survive. Of
course, the best organisations have always been doing it.

The case of Honda

Some of the greatest exponents of Ready – Fire – Aim as a learning cycle are
the Japanese. A study of the Honda entry into the US motorcycle business[1]
shows not only the Japanese ability to experiment, but to use their mistakes
to learn and build success.

The sales team from Honda arrived in the USA in 1959, ill prepared and ill
equipped for what was to follow. They were armed with a strategy that was
directed merely at seeing whether they could sell something in the United
States.

The management of Honda was sceptical about the whole project and limited
the cash allocation for the team, who therefore had to rent low-cost facilities
for warehousing and living. Their planning was so poor that they arrived in Los
Angeles at the end of the 1959 motorcycle sales season. They had to wait a
year for any sales to materialise. Then, as one of the managers in charge of
this experiment put it 'disaster struck'.

The motorcycles they had managed to sell began to leak oil and break down.
The conditions and riding style for motorcycles were different in the USA and
Japan. In Japan, motorcycles were essentially town vehicles, used for short
runs at low speed. In the USA motorcycles were ridden faster and for longer
periods on the open highway. The motorcycles were not designed for this
style of operation and began to break down. The sales team had to transfer
their attention from sales to repairs, and managed to stop the most serious
faults by patching and mending.

[1] Richard Pascale, 'Perspectives on strategy: the real story behind Honda's success', *Cali-
fornia Management Review*, Spring 1994; quoted in Henry Mintzberg, *Mintzberg on
Management*, The Free Press, 1989

At the same time they were learning what it takes to be a success in the marketplace. They had an idea (Ready), put it into practice (Fire) and were now analysing what went wrong in the implementation (Aim).

Just before they packed their bags to return to Japan, they tried another experiment. The planners in Japan had analysed the US market to some extent and found a predominance of larger machines. They had therefore reserved their larger motorcycles for the US market. (There was also the reason that Mr. Honda was especially fond of the 250 and 350cc machines. He thought that the handlebar shape was reminiscent of the eyebrow of Buddha, and was therefore a strong selling point.)

They took along some smaller 50cc Supercub machines (the largest selling machine in Japan) and used them for their own transport around Los Angeles. They had eliminated the Supercub from serious consideration in the market that was geared towards bigger and more luxurious machines. Eventually they were approached by Sears who wanted to sell the smaller bikes. The sales team refused on the grounds that they would upset the image that they were trying to create in the marketplace for larger machines.

Eventually they were forced into selling the 50cc bike when the bigger machines started to break down. The rest of the story is well known – Honda bikes began to sell, to the expense of the local motorcycle industry. They achieved their success not through a well-planned and perfectly executed strategy, but through making mistakes, trying things out, following hunches and ideas and learning all the time. All of their lessons about the US market in terms of customer preferences and the needs of the environment were translated with characteristic efficiency into improvements in their engineering and sales approach. A clear case of Ready – Fire – Aim.

Honda and some of their Japanese industrial colleagues are past masters of Ready – Fire – Aim as an innovative process. They collect customer information at an alarming level, and produce product enhancements and innovations at a startling rate. For example, Sony bring out 1,000 new products a year. That's an average of four new products for every working day. Some 80 per cent are improvements or enhancements to existing products — usually new features with better performance at a lower price. The other 20 per cent are aimed at totally new markets. They haven't lost their ability to experiment as a result of market dominance – they continue to learn from their experiences and are ready and able to make changes to their product line.

The story of the Honda success is repeated across Japanese industry. In the 1950s they had the reputation for cheap and shoddy goods, mere copies of their western counterparts. Some 20 years later they were the market leaders in many of these industries and were continuing to make improvements and introduce innovations that surpassed anything that the West had to offer. Now they dominate most industry sectors.

Harnessing innovation

If Ready – Fire – Aim is a way to innovate, and if most ideas come from the people that already work for you, then capturing these ideas is of paramount importance to any organisation.

The case of the suggestion scheme

Most companies have a suggestion scheme. In many cases this is a small box on the wall of the canteen that is emptied of its contents infrequently. At best, serious suggestions receive an acknowledgement but little action – the scheme falls into disrepute and the suggestions degenerate into what management can do with their suggestion scheme!

Some suggestion schemes give cash awards to employees based on the contribution that their improvement made to the company. Derisory payments in comparison to the savings made, or lengthy arguments within the organisation as to the eligibility of the employee for an award lead these schemes into further problems. Publicising major savings has the effect of limiting suggestions as employees feel that their minor improvement is not going to receive consideration — the impression is that the company is only looking for big numbers.

The final death-knell for the suggestion scheme is the 'Not Invented Here' syndrome which precludes any idea for improvement coming from a worker in another discipline or function, and endless committees and delays in adjudication consigns the scheme to the same fate as the earlier example – total disinterest and misuse.

Contrast this all too common experience with the experience in some Japanese organisations. Here the concept of participation and continuous improvement ideas coming from the workforce is part of the culture, not an add-on scheme. Everyone feels the right and the need to participate. Half of the companies in a survey of schemes in Japan had participation rates over 90 per cent. Recognition is given for the idea contribution, not the financial worth of the proposal. Suggestions are not of major economic benefit. The average is about £90 in Japan as against an average of £5,000 per proposal in similar US schemes.[2]

[2] Yuzo Yasuda, *40 Years, 20 Million Ideas*, Productivity Press, 1991

The Toyota Creative Idea Suggestion Scheme is the benchmark example. In its early development in the 1950s the Toyota suggestion scheme looked pretty standard: 5,000 or so suggestions a year, a participation rate of about 16 per cent. Out of these suggestions, only about 30 per cent were implemented.

In 1981, some 30 years after the scheme was started at Toyota, the number of suggestions had increased to nearly 2 million per year; an average of over 30 suggestions per worker of which 95 per cent were implemented. By 1986 the suggestion average was running at 47.7 suggestions per person per year, and participation was at 94 per cent of the workforce. (An average British suggestion scheme participation rate in 1993 was 10 per cent,[3] 3 in the USA the average was 12 per cent.[4])

This level of innovative activity has come through hard work in making the scheme work and in developing a culture that thrives on innovation and values people's suggestions. Can it work in Western companies? The answer is yes, but with reservations. Although Land Rover have been consistently growing their suggestion scheme over the last 10 years, they are a long way behind the Toyota numbers. But they do compare well against the poor British average of one suggestion per 10 employees with a figure of 3.2 suggestions per worker in 1992.

Where the comparison still falls down even further is in implementation. At Toyota, 95 per cent of ideas are implemented, at Land Rover the figure is 13 per cent. Western organisations still seem less willing to experiment and take risks than their Japanese counterparts.

There are many similar success stories to be found in other Western organisations, but they tend to exist in pockets of excellence.[5] The examples are still not widespread and the culture of innovation is not robust.

The case of Art Fry and the Post-It Note

The Post-It Note has become one of the essential products in the office of today. So popular have the little yellow (and now rainbow coloured) stickers become that some managers have tried – and failed – to ban their use. Their complaint is that there are often so many Post-It Notes pasted to a document

[3] UK Association of Suggestion Schemes, quoted in *Personal Management Plus*, April 1993

[4] National Association of Suggestion Schemes survey, 1987

[5] For a detailed study of innovative approaches in a number of industrial and service organisations see Tom Peters and Nancy Austin, *A Passion for Excellence*, Random House, 1985, and Tom Peters, *Thriving on Chaos*, Excel, 1987

that you cannot even see the original text! But whether you like them or not, you cannot fail to recognise that this little sticky note is a phenomenal money spinner for its originating organisation, 3M, and it is one of the biggest success stories of the modern era.

But it was not a straightforward innovation like the Swatch watch, where a niche was created and exploited with relative ease. It took twelve years for the product idea to be developed to a commercial success. Twelve years of experimentation, learning, adapting and trying something out again. Twelve years of Ready – Fire – Aim.

The story of the development starts with the development of an adhesive that does not work and a choir member whose hymn book markers kept on falling out. Art Fry was a researcher at 3M, the maker of Scotch tape and sundry other adhesive and coating products. He was frustrated that his paper markers kept on falling out of his music books and longed for a piece of paper that he could stick to the page, but one that would not tear or leave a mark when it was removed.

At the same research centre an adhesive was developed that didn't stick very well – a failure in most people's eyes who were working for an adhesive manufacturer. But it was not a failure to Art Fry – it was exactly the product that he was seeking. He was now able to mark his place without damaging the book, and without fear of the marker falling out. He was on to a winner – for other frustrated choir members.

73

The Ready – Fire – Aim process was already underway, and was cycled through a few times to perfect the right mix and style for the marker paper. Fry thought of using the sticker for other purposes in the office. But no one was interested. Major office suppliers thought that the idea was silly and refused to even consider stocking the product. The product developers at 3M did not see the value or potential of a product for which there was no demand. The project died several times.

Eventually, Fry went round the executive and management secretaries at 3M and gave them the Post-It Notes to use. They loved the idea and started to demand them. That only created an internal market. Then, under the signature of the Chief Executive Officer (CEO) of 3M, Post-It Notes were mailed to every CEO's secretary in the Fortune 500. The result was the same as for the 3M secretaries. Demand grew, and the office equipment suppliers were being asked to supply the notes. Post-It Notes are now a $200 million plus business for 3M.

For most of the time of this twelve-year development in 3M, the project had no official status or funding. It was, in the terminology of Tom Peters, a 'skunkwork' – a project that existed on the edge of the organisation, being funded from other agreed projects, and being sustained through the belief of a champion, in this instance Art Fry.

Except in organisations like 3M, where 'skunkwork' is the norm, these innovative projects are rare. The desire for control and order in most Western organisations has knocked out most innovation from the process. And yet it is the lack of creativity and innovation that are often the rallying cries of many a Chairman or Managing Director talking about the problems of industry today.

Killing ideas

Our cultures have been so ingrained with the need to produce something right and not to make mistakes that the idea is stillborn. There is a blinkered approach that assumes that you cannot produce any new product without an extensive period of research and development. There is an accepted engineering assumption that model changes and new products take time to perfect and bring to the market – there is no other way. The belief is so strongly held that people fail to see what is happening in their own marketplace. They do not see the reality. They are blinded by their own assumptions and perception.

So even when a breakthrough occurs in the approach, the Ready – Fire – Aim model is often misused. The top of the organisation preaches the messages of change, continuous improvement and learning from mistakes. Task forces are set up, training undertaken and problems investigated. But when the first suggestion emerges that it is the management processes that are wrong – when the changes need to be at the top as well as the bottom of the organisation – then top management reverts to type. They still use the Ready – Fire – Aim model, but now the Aim – Fire process is directed at the people who are doing the criticising, the people who have been foolish enough to believe that the culture had changed. The messengers are shot, along with the 'Japanese' processes, and the organisation reverts to its previous ways, with enormous relief.

Ready – Fire – Aim in its successful innovation mode is not a concept that fits well into the traditional hierarchies of the West. Organisation leaders are past masters at rationalisation and cover-up. They seek to minimise risk and to hide errors and therefore not learn from them, covering up any traces of a faulty decision making process. When there is a rare success from an accident or experiment, managers are equally masterful at showing how this was achieved through long and detailed planning and research.

Inappropriate ideas

Ready – Fire – Aim is the way to develop new approaches and innovate, but there is a danger – identifying the right idea to develop. Ready – Fire – Aim often works in our organisations by implementing inappropriate ideas. As we have seen earlier, there is a bias towards action, even in a perfectly balanced problem-solving team. There are more Fire oriented roles than Ready or Aim. Thus when a new idea does come into the frame, the action people will often race ahead into implementation without thinking. The process is often just Ready – Fire. Once again, the Aim often comes by way of a post-mortem on a failure, usually directed at finding a scapegoat rather than learning from the process.

The case of the improvement team

A major oil company, along with most of its rivals and competitors in the industry, had begun a process of change and improvement in their working practices. This was partly as a result of pressure from their parent organisation who were pursuing a global quality-improvement initiative, and also in order to stay competitive and to lengthen the working life of some of their operations in the North Sea. Part of this process of change was to try to involve their employees more in decisions that affected them. To push decisions further down the hierarchy and to reduce the bureaucracy that had grown up over the years of their success.

Some minor areas of activity were chosen for pilot schemes in employee involvement. One of these was the specification and purchase of protective clothing. As anyone who has worked in industry at or near to the shop floor will know, the whole question of the adequacy, design and availability of protective clothing is a major area of conflict between management and workers. Due to the large sums of money involved and the corporate image implications, the decisions on design and supply have been jealously guarded by management and purchasing officers. The clothing that is supplied is often inadequate for the job. In these situations the last person to be asked for their opinion, and the person who can offer most, is the person who actually uses the clothing.

So, the company decided to form a small team to investigate the supply and design of the new issue of protective clothing, thus demonstrating its support of employee involvement in a very contentious arena. The team was put together from a cross-section of interested parties and comprised operators, supervisors and other staff who were involved with the supply and issue of protective clothing, including safety and purchasing representatives.

The team set off with characteristic enthusiasm, collecting data about cus-

75

tomer wants and supplier capabilities. Very soon they discovered a new material being supplied by a Dutch manufacturer with some unique capabilities. It was a fire-retarding and static-dispersing material that was also light in weight and affordable. Most fire-retarding materials are either heavy, hot or expensive (often all three). As the team was specifying clothing for off-shore oil workers in the aftermath of the Piper Alpha disaster and other fire-related accidents in the area, the qualities of fire retardency and static dispersing were of very high value from a safety perspective.

Finding this material available, the team quickly went on to present their proposal to management, who were suitably impressed with the way their new devolved decision making process was operating. This was a great example of innovation and empowerment in action – the team had been given a task, they had researched it well, found an innovative solution and they hadn't taken too long to do it. The proposal was quickly agreed and the team proceeded to implement their proposal – to equip all personnel with clothing made from this new material with immediate effect.

The clothing was all made to measure, personalised with the individual's name embroidered on the breast pocket and delivered. The team and the company were congratulating themselves on their success when one of the managers who received his clothing noticed something wrong.

The new material had a titanium fibre in the weave. This provided some of its qualities of static dispersal and fire retardance. However, it also was a metal and could conduct electricity. The protective clothing would be worn by electricians and other maintenance workers often working on live circuits. In the words of the manager 'It would be like wrapping them up in tin foil.' The clothing was withdrawn. (Out of interest – this manager was one of the only Evaluators in the whole organisation.)

The organisation had followed Ready – Fire – Aim, but with costly side effects. They had fallen in love with a new idea and had failed to investigate it properly in a pilot process before moving to full implementation. Their bias as an organisation was towards action, to Fire. Their only change had been to add the Ready stage to their familiar culture.

Summary

The Ready – Aim – Fire organisation seems to be the blueprint for the 1990s. It is loved by the management gurus for its constant innovation and questioning of the status quo. It is the flexible and adaptive organisation that meets the challenges of the rapidly changing world and exploits the discontinuities to best effect.

But Ready – Aim – Fire can also be a dangerous concept to add onto a traditional management culture. Then it becomes a slogan rather than a process, and ill-conceived ideas are implemented in the name of innovation. The traditional approach of 'one right way' and 'no mistakes' does not marry well with experimentation and learning from errors. Instead of rapid experimentation and pilot programmes, full scale change is tried, with disastrous results. The management culture then reverts to its original process, having proved conclusively that the new way 'won't work here'.

Most suggestion schemes and innovation initiatives fail after 12 – 18 months effort due to the lack of commitment of management. In this time frame it is still too comfortable to revert to the old way of working and very difficult to learn the new ways. Managers will therefore try to find every opportunity to sabotage the effort and prove the old way is best, therefore avoiding the need to change.

The learning is again one of balance. A total move to Ready – Fire – Aim is not possible, or desirable for most organisations and industries. But there is a need to have an innovation culture in order to survive in the turbulent economic and business environment. In order to succeed an overall vision and strategy for the organisation that allows for innovation needs to be set and supported by management. Then the projects and suggestion schemes can be set up with the knowledge that there is the management commitment to make them work through the difficult first few months. Then the sort of success that is evident from the innovative organisations such as 3M, Honda, Land Rover, Toyota and Sony can be gained.

8

The 'Fire – Fire – Fire' organisation

Don't think – act

Ready – Fire – Aim is the innovative organisation, Ready – Ready – Ready is the creative organisation. Fire – Fire – Fire is the action organisation. Many organisations have a culture of action. It is in the nature of the balance of the team roles, that even if the team or organisation is perfectly balanced, there is a majority of action oriented roles – people who want to stop the talking and get into action. Individuals with a Judging bias will also be action oriented, especially those who have a Sensing preference as well. The SJ combination makes for a traditional, stabilising influence in an organisation, decisive and acting within established rules and procedures. Impatient with delays and intolerant of anyone who wishes to take a new or innovative look at a situation or problem.

Organisations in the recent economic environment have listened to the gurus of innovation and creativity, but have tended to follow a short-term view in order to placate the stockholder's desire for profit and return on investment. The desire is for action. However, organisations and individuals are so keen to do something, to be active, that they will almost do anything to keep busy. It often seems to be more important to be active than to think about what to do. Jumping into action often hides what the real problem is.

The primary objective in organisation success is for people to do the right things and to do them right. The assumption is that when there are mistakes — when a product is faulty, when there is a customer complaint, when the budget is exceeded — people are doing the right things but getting them wrong. Therefore managers put all of their effort into establishing further controls and procedures to ensure that it is done right in the future. They miss the point that all of the quality management experts have been trying to point out for years: people are not Luddites, they are doing things right most of the time, but they are doing the wrong things. The process causes the mistakes. In surveys across industry, over 80 per cent of the mistakes come from people doing the wrong things right. The difficulty is that in an action oriented organisation, there is no time to analyse the process and see what is wrong — the reaction is to jump into action and treat the effect not the cause.

The case of the incorrectly spelt report

An international research organisation was very successful in breaking into the lucrative Japanese market. The organisation was famed for its quality assurance procedures. It provided a good service and tried to be close to the customer. In all respects, it seemed a model for success. Then came the bombshell from its major Japanese client in the form of a comment: 'If you persist in sending us reports that have words that are incorrectly spelt, we will take our business elsewhere.'

79

They were suffering from the syndrome reported by an airline executive some years ago – 'Coffee stains on the flip-down tables suggest that you don't do your engine maintenance correctly.' At this research company, the tangible output of their process was the report to the customer — a written document that detailed the findings of their eighteen-month to two-year research projects. The Japanese client had made the assumption that if they were slipshod with their reports, then they might also be slipshod with their science.

The management team were almost entirely SJ types, and with Implementer, Coordinator or Driver role preferences. When faced with any problem, let alone a crisis as serious as this one, the response was Fire – Fire – Fire. Without any real analysis of the problem, the management team went into action. An outside agency was engaged, at great cost, to proof-read every report that left the organisation. The reports were lengthy and complex, so this would be no easy task.

This was the traditional response of this organisation — jump into action and fix the problem. By chance, a Total Quality Management project was under way at the same time in the company, so the TQM manager decided to do some analysis work (using the TQM credo of making decisions based on facts not feelings). Very quickly, he discovered that the typists were not using the spell-check software on their word processors. In some cases they did not know that there was a spell-check program – it had not been included in their training. In other cases, they knew about the spell-check, but did not use it under the mistaken belief that it was frowned upon by senior management (who had joked that it was a lazy way to spell.)

In either case, the spell-check was not being used. The simple process of putting the reports through the spell-check program eliminated some 85 per cent of the errors. The Japanese client was satisfied with the reaction, but more importantly with the methodology used and the promise of continual improvement thereafter. The company saved a very important client relationship, saved money in not using a proof-reader, learned to Aim before Firing, and learned to apply a process of problem solving rather than to leap into action.

The company had also learned that mistakes come from doing the wrong things right — all of the typists were following their understanding of the procedures and putting in their best efforts. They were not trying to make mistakes. It was the process they were using that was at fault. Subsequent improvements in the process reduced the level of errors in reports even more. To have retained the proof-reader would not have addressed the cause of the errors.

Busy work

A further implication of doing wrong things right is that people do not question the process, which is usually laid down by management and tradition, and is therefore inviolate in many people's eyes who are supporters of tradition and stability (the SJ type again). Studies of Western industry from the 1950s onward have all highlighted the enormous waste that exists due to people doing 'busy' work. That is, they are following procedures and processes blindly, not questioning whether there is any value in the work they are doing.

The case of the construction project

A major multinational company was investing millions of pounds in a new production line. External contractors were carrying out the construction and the liaison with suppliers of plant and equipment. Internal company engineers were providing the management of the project.

The project was several months behind schedule, and the position was getting worse. The management decided to call in a computerised project management system to help with the planning process. The hardware and software was duly purchased, and a small team established to transfer the manual schedules on to the computer system. Within a few days the system was operational and the project manager had a system to help him manage the project and get it back on to schedule.

Weeks later, the progress against the plan had not improved, in fact it had got worse. The project was falling further behind in both time and cost estimates, despite extra resources being allocated to its management. A hint at the cause of the problem came from one of the weekly progress meetings between the project managers and the key contractor staff.

Before each meeting a detailed print-out of the schedule was produced by the computerised system. Project management charts showed each part of the project, the interdependencies, the time-scale and the due completion date. At the meeting, the Project Manager went down the critical path analysis for that day — very little of the activity that was planned for completion had been finished. But instead of using the information to highlight a potential problem and to try to rectify the situation to bring the schedule back into line, the manager merely took down a new estimate of the completion date. This new information was then fed into the computer that printed out new project management charts and schedules by the end of the day.

The manager had not been managing the project to completion, he had been rescheduling the project on a weekly basis. He was following the procedure that was laid down by his bosses who had introduced the computer system. They believed that the way to get the project back on track was to improve the scheduling and reporting. All that did in fact was to add another procedure to an ineffective management process and divert attention from the real issue.

81

The project management computer system was very efficient in producing the project management charts and project information, it was not effective in managing the project. The difference between efficiency and effectiveness is clear in many other organisation processes. All sectors of the economy are riddled with practices that cause people to do the wrong things right. The Project Manager on the construction project was managing the computerised information system very well – he was doing it right. But he was doing the wrong thing by abdicating the day-to-day control of the project to the computer. He was too busy following procedures and carrying out the wishes of his bosses to step back and think about what he was doing.

Procedures and processes have been built up over the years through custom and practice. Once they are written down, they are incredibly difficult to change, despite the changes in the environment. Trade union members have known for years that the best way of ensuring that a company ceases to operate is to 'Work to Rule' – to follow to the letter the written and agreed processes for working. These are usually so contradictory that it is impossible for the business to function. Years of Fire – Fire – Fire has caused a plethora of rules, agreements and practices to be drawn up and agreed to satisfy the immediate need. No thought was put into how they affected each other, the most important need was to get the plant back into operation, at any cost.

In the 1970s and 1980s these inefficient practices, coupled with the increasing global competition from the emerging industrial nations of Japan and its neighbours, caused the demise of many famous names. Even more industries are still fighting the traditions and cultures of the earlier years using Total Quality Management, participative management or re-engineering to re-draw the work patterns and eliminate the waste. All of these methodologies have in common the use of a systematic approach to problem solving that questions the status quo, identifies new ways of working, evaluates these new ways to elicit the best solution and then implement these solutions – a Ready – Aim – Fire process.

For most companies, the missing steps are Ready and Aim. There is usually a lack of creativity in thinking about new ways of doing things. Any spark is quickly put out by comments like – 'we've always done it this way' – 'we tried that before and it didn't work' – 'it just won't work here' – 'there's only one way to do this'. People are not used to thinking about processes and improvement. They are also so keen to move into action that they omit to think about what they are doing. We have seen how this bias to action causes dangerous situations in a Ready – Fire – Aim process. But for many organisations there is no danger of pursuing a dangerous new idea because there are no new ideas. They are stuck in Fire – Fire – Fire.

The case of the consultancy firm

The consultancy arm of one of the top international accountancy practices wanted to develop their client/consultant team working. As a result of analysis work carried out on their preferred roles and working practice, it was evident that everyone was action oriented. They all had preferred roles of Driver, Implementer or Coordinator.

When questioned about their working practices, the consultant team identified that this action orientation followed through into their client work. Like most of the large professional practices, they had targets to reach on their own time that was billable to clients. In this particular case, the target was over 80 per cent of consultants' time should be billed to clients. This pushed them into a working process of always being active – not reflecting on, or thinking about, what they were doing.

As consultants, they were always on a project, or even connected to several projects at the same time. Whether they were on a client's premises or in their own office the need was to be active, and to appear to be working hard. Reports that came from the teams were comprehensive and weighty. Regular project team meetings allocated tasks and kept the project leaders up to date with progress. Management pressure kept everyone, including the project leaders, well aware of the need to meet billing targets and pursue an aggressive stance on non-attributed costs.

The culture was clear – be busy. Unfortunately this usually meant be busy on anything, whether it was useful or not. The clients' needs were often forgotten in the drive to turn out reports and recommendations and to bill as soon as possible to keep a positive cash flow.

The group reflected on what their customers wanted from their consultancy service. The consensus was that clients wanted two things – new ideas for their problems, and critical evaluation of their current practices and activities. Ready and Aim. The balance of the teams working on these projects was Fire – Fire – Fire. They did not have anyone who could match the needs of the clients. Those few people in the organisation who had creative or evaluative roles were looked upon as oddities and misfits. They found themselves constantly at odds with their project team leaders and were regularly reassigned.

The problem is understandable – the consulting firm was in the same position as industry in the success years of the immediate post-war period in the Western economies. The demand for products (now for consultancy services) was so high that there was little real competition and the successful firms developed a degree of complacency. As Tom Peters commented 'You couldn't screw up Fortune 500 company in the 1950s and 60s if you tried.'[1] In industry you didn't need to think or innovate that much. The consumer was not used to having new products available, and there was little competition. All you had to do was to keep the production lines turning at all costs. Industries would rather exploit the declining technology rather than utilise new (and potentially risky) technologies.

To do this you recruited people who were keen to get on and do things, to solve problems quickly, and to keep the wheels turning. They in turn recruited more people to fill their positions who looked like them, and the self-fulfilling cycle continued. By the time the world changed, these organisations had developed such internally focused cultures that they were isolated from reality. They just did not see what was happening. For example, Xerox allowed the Japanese to enter the photocopier market through small models and personal

[1] Tom Peters in *A Passion for Excellence* video, Video Publishing House

copiers, assuming that they could still hold on to the market through the power of their history and their relative size.

Today's reality for the manufacturing business, the public sector utility and the consulting firm is that the marketplace is changing so rapidly that complacency means going out of business. Many firms were not as successful as Xerox, NCR or British Airways in making a radical turnaround in the face of disaster — they went out of business or are still struggling to survive. Fire – Fire – Fire is great if you don't have to cope with change.

Just make it work

A final example of the Fire – Fire – Fire organisation again highlights the desire to be in action and busy. This time not just jumping to conclusions and implementing inappropriate solutions (almost a Ready – Fire process), and not just being busy following outdated procedures. The action orientation applied to, say, an engineering operation makes people try to make something work because it is there.

In the former Soviet Union, US and British firms, thrown out after the revolution in 1917, have been amazed to return to their factories in the 1990s to find original machinery still working, long after it had been scrapped in the West. One US organisation wanted to ship a complete factory back to its museum in the States as they had no examples of the machines in the museum — and these machines were still in everyday use in 1993! These are examples of the 'make it work' philosophy abound in situations where isolation and crisis conditions require it for survival. Often a degree of innovation is found, but the essential process is action centred.

The case of the engineering plant

At a major process engineering facility, a number of pieces of equipment were installed to improve the process. They had all been tried out and tested at other locations, and in other situations. The technology was not new, it was merely applying it to a similar process.

From the outset, some of the pieces of equipment did not work very well. Not that they were faulty or broke down – they just didn't do the task that they were designed for as effectively as they did in other facilities. As the machines were of proven reliability and efficiency, the management and maintenance crews on the new plant were determined to make the machines work. The implication was that they could not run them as well as their colleagues.

For years they continued to try to make them work as well as at other sites, continuing to modify, repair, improve, monitor and maintain them. They invested thousands of pounds of new money to try and make the original investment work. Eventually, a new manager identified that the environment was so different that the machines would never work to design capacity. They had been designed for one set of conditions, and were totally unsuited to conditions in another part of the same industry.

The action orientation of the management and engineers had stopped them from standing back from the problem and analysing the total environment and process – they merely solved the immediate problem, every day.

The managers in the above case were stuck in a Fire – Fire – Fire process of troubleshooting, fire fighting not fire prevention. The 'get it done', 'don't ask questions', 'production at all costs', 'make it work' philosophy that permeates a lot of manufacturing and production companies has diverted the Aim focus away from the real problem to the myriad of little problems that present themselves every day. The wood is missed by looking at all of the trees.

85

Summary

Fire – Fire – Fire is the disease of many Western organisations and the symptom of many of our managers. The action orientation is valued in many ways by our society which idolises the charismatic leader and troubleshooter, entering a situation with guns blazing and putting wrongs to right with a minimum of fuss. Our organisations have wanted to recruit people with leadership qualities, those who are quick to take up the reins in open situations, those who are decisive. Our traditional structures and culture have established policies and procedures that can run into many volumes, to be added to by successive revisions and updates.

All of these factors go to make up the organisation that tries to respond and causes more problems; the organisation where everyone is busy and where nothing gets done; the organisation where fixing it is a virtue, whether it is needed or not. There is a need to get things done, but not at any cost. What the Fire – Fire – Fire organisation requires is a direction in which to direct its energy. Effective implementation follows a strategy developed by balancing Fire with the creative input of Ready and the critical evaluation of Aim.

In all of the cases and examples of this and the previous chapters, the need for a balance has been highlighted. In the following chapters we will look at how to achieve that balance through the use of tools and techniques and by developing your individual skills. As previously identified in an individual context, a weakness can often be an overuse or misuse of a strength. The same is true in an organisational context, the strength of a particular organisation approach can also be its weakness, especially when the environment changes. The successful organisation will learn to be flexible by continually scanning its environment and balancing its strengths and compensating for its shortcomings in relation to the current needs of that environment. The need to be creative, innovative, cautious and action oriented at the right time.

9

Balancing the process

Balancing a team using team roles

Each of the individual team roles has a real value to the successful working of the team, and the absence of any one of them will weaken the team. Equally, the presence of more than one person in a role, or an overly strong person in one role can produce imbalances which can cause the team to be not as successful as possible. The ideal team is one where each of the team roles is strongly represented by one person, and everyone in the team understands and values the contribution and role of each other. R. Meredith Belbin's original research and subsequent practical application of the principles in real work situations has proved over and over again that the balanced team will out-perform any other team composition. It is this balance therefore that we are seeking.

Not many of us are in a position to choose our colleague team members, whether we are in a position of power or not in an organisation. It is only in the instances of setting up green-field operations and new project teams that the opportunity arises, and even then the constraints of availability of suitable people and timing will inevitably condition our choice to something less than ideal.

Equally, we may be in situations where we have more or less than eight members in our team. Or we may be involved with a number of different teams where the task and balance is different. There are a number of questions that arise almost immediately when one begins to analyse the team roles: How do I balance an existing team? What about teams where there are fewer than eight members? Are there situations where a less than perfect balance is appropriate? What if I am in a number of different teams where the needs are different?

Balancing existing teams

The process of balancing starts with the awareness of the current balance of team roles in the team, and an acceptance of the worth of each role to the successful performance of the team. A more detailed analysis of each individual's preferred roles can then help in creating an ideal mix, in particular by looking at the secondary preferences. Often by using the secondary preferences, a balance can be obtained with the team members then contracting to use these designated roles in team activities.

The case of the Alpha Project team

The Alpha project team completed the team role inventory and posted their scores on a flipchart (Table 9.1).

The team looked at their preferred roles, and immediately noticed an obvious skewing towards the Implementer role, with three of them recording this as their preferred role. Next, they observed that there was no Evaluator, and no Creator. They would lack creative input, relying heavily on George as the Investigator to provide the Ready input. The tendency for the team would be to move too quickly into implementation without gathering sufficient information and without any evaluation – the potential was to Fire – Fire – Fire.

The team were keen to follow a Ready – Aim – Fire approach with a balanced team, so they next looked at the second preferences in each inventory and added them to the flipchart. (Table 9.2). Very quickly they noticed that they could achieve a balanced team as the team members had second preferences that included Creator and Evaluator. They asked John to take up his secondary role of Creator instead of the duplicated role of Implementer, and asked Ros to use her secondary role of Evaluator instead of Implementer. They now had a balanced team.

Both Ros and Robin had secondary roles of Evaluator and primary roles of Implementer. In asking Ros instead of Robin to make the change, the team took into account the closeness of the scores on the inventory between the primary and secondary roles. In Robin's case there was a large difference – he scored very highly on Implementer, and then had a large gap to a cluster of scores with Evaluator the top. Ros, on the other hand had her scores for Implementer and Evaluator within a couple of points of each other as clear preferences, then with a large gap to the other role scores. So it would be easier for Ros to change her role than for Robin to change his. The closer the scores on the inventory, the easier it is to move between the roles. The wider the scores are apart, the more difficult it is to change roles.

So the Alpha team had managed to balance their team with very little effort. Your team may not be as easy to balance, but the process

Table 9.1

THE ALPHA PROJECT TEAM ROLES

Name	Preferred role
ROS	IMPLEMENTER
ROBIN	IMPLEMENTER
ALICE	COMMUNICATOR
GEORGE	INVESTIGATOR
JOHN	IMPLEMENTER
ISABELLE	FINISHER
ANDREW	DRIVER
DANIEL	COORDINATOR

Table 9.2

THE ALPHA TEAM BALANCE

Name	Primary role	Secondary role
ROS	IMPLEMENTER	EVALUATOR
ROBIN	IMPLEMENTER	EVALUATOR
ALICE	COMMUNICATOR	IMPLEMENTER
GEORGE	INVESTIGATOR	CREATOR
JOHN	IMPLEMENTER	CREATOR
ISABELLE	FINISHER	COORDINATOR
ANDREW	DRIVER	COORDINATOR
DANIEL	COORDINATOR	IMPLEMENTER

followed by the Alpha team is reasonably successful in that it shares the information and allows everyone to recognise where the possible failings in the problem-solving process might be. You should attempt to at least balance the Ready – Aim – Fire process by having someone who can speak for that part of the process in the team.

It is not easy to change one's preferred role. It needs concentrated effort and the support of other team members to achieve results. You can assist the learning and change by using the Counselling Notes for each role which appear at the end of this chapter. These counselling notes identify the positive and negative behaviours associated with each of the roles and can be used to help you develop a specific role, or to coach others in their development process.

What if no one in the team has a secondary preference to fill the gap?

The case of the Beta Project team

The Alpha team had an easy solution to their imbalance. The Beta team has a more difficult problem. They charted their primary and secondary preferences and still find that they have no one who can fulfil the Ready roles of Creator or Investigator. As their team project is one that requires innovation, they have a problem. Their team is overwhelmingly action oriented, and has a further problem in having three individuals with a Driver preference.

Table 9.3

THE BETA TEAM ROLES

Name	Primary role	Secondary role
CHARLES	IMPLEMENTER	EVALUATOR
PETER	DRIVER	EVALUATOR
KIRSTY	COMMUNICATOR	IMPLEMENTER
ALAN	DRIVER	FINISHER
ROSEMARY	IMPLEMENTER	COORDINATOR
KATE	IMPLEMENTER	COORDINATOR
PIERRE	DRIVER	IMPLEMENTER
CHRIS	COORDINATOR	IMPLEMENTER

As a first step, the Beta team recognised the difficulty of having three Drivers. There is a strong potential for conflict between them when competing for the task leadership of the team. So, Peter agreed to take on the role of Evaluator and Alan the role of Finisher for the team. Both recognised that this would be difficult as their secondary roles were not very close in the inventory scores, but both agreed that it was possible provided the rest of the team gave them support and feedback on their behaviour. Pierre had an even greater difference between his primary and secondary roles, and the secondary role of implementer was not in short supply. Kirsty, in her role as Communicator agreed to take on a coaching role for team and to watch closely for any development of conflict between Peter, Alan and Pierre and the rest of the team.

When it came to introducing the Ready roles, three possible solutions were considered: they could look at third preference roles; they could look to bring in expertise from outside the team; or they could fill the gap by agreeing a process and using a creative problem solving technique.

They evaluated each option carefully, with Peter taking the lead to practise his Evaluator behaviours. First, they considered if someone could fill the roles using a third or lower preference role. They decided against this option as it presents problems to that person in terms of assimilating the role, and being able to play it firmly in the team. The only way that this could work is if the person has a small score difference across a number of roles. No one fell into that category, so the effort to fill the role would be too great.

Secondly, they looked to import the expertise from outside the team when needed. They considered asking a colleague or consultant to join the team for the Ready part of the process. This was a more feasible option for the team as there were several people to choose from who could take on the role. However, they felt their overall objective to come up with an innovative solution was such that they needed to have a permanent focus on the creative skills, not just for a short period.

91

The third option that they evaluated was that the team itself takes on collective responsibility for the gap and agrees to use a process and a technique to aid their thinking. As their purpose was innovation, and they all recognised the imbalance of the team, they agreed that this was the best course of action for them. They agreed that they should take some group action on creative inputs and to use techniques such as brainstorming (see Chapter 14) to generate the ideas and options. They had all used these techniques before, so they felt confident that they could follow the process, but in order to get off to a good start, they decided to invite a consultant to join the first two team meetings to lead them in some training exercises and to facilitate their first deliberations on the problem.

The Beta team shared their problem of imbalance and discovered a solution that suited their needs and the personal preferences within the team. Other teams need to consider their own unique situation and individual preferences to decide which of the options, or combination of options, is best for them.

What if there are fewer than eight members in the team?

If there are fewer than eight in a team, members can double up and perform two of the functions instead of one. When deciding who can best double up in the team, then you need to take note of the strength of preference for each role in each individual. Someone who has a very strong tendency for one role will find it difficult to perform a secondary function, someone whose primary and secondary role scores are close together will find it easy to move between the two. So the best balance will come from people taking on roles that they can effectively move between rather than just taking on a second role for the sake of equality. That may mean that the best option is for someone to take on three roles, and another member to stay with one.

When looking at balance in a small team, the Ready – Aim – Fire balance is the first important step. After that, the options are to double up roles; to import the role; and to use a technique to cover the gap. Once again the best option may be a combination of these three options, as demonstrated by the Beta team example.

Where there are more than eight in a team, the team members need to agree who is going to provide the primary focus in the role. Here the person with the highest preference score, or the largest gap between primary and secondary scores would be the first choice as they would find it difficult to suppress their strong preference.

Are there times when a less than perfect balance is appropriate?

The Belbin research suggested that the balanced team would work more effectively in any situation. Certainly, having all of the team role skills available is an asset, but some of the roles could be more important than others in different business applications. In a fast-moving, rapidly changing environment the Creator role is more important than it is in a stable continuous process operation with no need for innovation. Different roles can be more critical in other situations. If a team decides that an deliberate imbalance is appropriate, they must be aware of the potential dangers as well as the advantages. We have seen in the previous chapters the potential benefits, and the corresponding pitfalls, of Ready – Fire – Aim, Ready – Ready – Ready, and Fire – Fire – Fire.

What if you are a member of more than one team?

The research suggests that the team role is a preference that individuals take with them in whatever team they are working. However, the needs of different team balances may mean that you have to take on a different role in that team. Ros, the Alpha team member who switched to her secondary role of Evaluator from her primary preference of Implementer in the Alpha team balance has been asked to be a member of the Project Audit Team. This team has the function of overseeing the projects of the organisation and evaluating their progress against the developmental projections. There is a strong tendency toward Evaluating and Finishing within that team, with a distinct lack of organisation and scheduling. Ros finds that there is no one with a primary role of Implementer in the team. Someone has been trying to fulfil that role from a poor secondary score, but the overwhelming bias towards Aiming has meant that the team has not achieved a great deal. In this situation, Ros finds that she can use her primary role of Implementer to good effect and help the team towards a balance between evaluating the projects and implementing some recommendations.

Ros is therefore changing her roles dependent on the team need. Whilst we have a preference, the roles are not written on tablets of stone, and they can change over time, either through exposure to different needs or by conscious developmental effort. Awareness of the purpose and value of each of the different roles will make it easier for an individual to change between roles as the need arises.

Each team has its own unique needs based on the resources it has available, and its task. If someone is a member of more than one team (and we all are in one sense – a member of the work team, the department team, and the company team), then a separate balancing process should be carried out in each team with clear contracts made between the team members regarding their roles. Again the use of the Counselling Notes will assist you to develop the necessary flexibility.

Knowledge of the different roles that individuals prefer is of vital importance to those empowered with making decisions over the make-up of management and project teams, as they can ensure a balance from the outset. However, the limited resources available and the general cultural bias of the organisation will mean that a perfectly balanced team is a rare animal. When trying to balance a team or when working with an established imbalanced group, you cannot expect miracles, and you cannot reorganise overnight. The key starting point is to make the team members aware of the roles, their purpose and their value to the team decision making process. Thus each individual can take on responsibility for carrying out their own team role effectively, and also the team can take steps to fill any gaps in the balance. The raising of awareness and valuing of the different roles and functions is 90 per cent of the journey to achieving the balance, and the sharing of the data is a useful team-building exercise in its own right.

Role counselling notes

These notes are designed to address the two main issues experienced by the individual team member or leader, with or without expert assistance in the counselling and coaching function.

For most of us the two issues are as follows. First, not being in a position to choose the team members. Mostly the members of teams are predetermined by other factors, not the least of them being a management and career development structure not run on Belbin parameters. How then can the leader and team aspire to obtain the undoubted benefits of the balanced team, when she or he must work with the existing people?

Secondly, our own personal development. How can we refine our personal team role to become more effective both individually and as a team member? Many team members wish to develop their role, and even develop secondary roles to enhance their own personal influence and effectiveness in the team, or to fit in with the needs of other teams where they are a member. Leaders have a voracious appetite in this area, wishing to fill any gaps and needs themselves, by being flexible in their role. Indeed, the leader is in the prime position to provide the flexibility, as she or he has the overall vision of the needs and the mission of the team.

The notes are set out as a description of each of the roles, with the behaviours associated with the role. By using and practising the 'Behaviours to be cultivated', individuals can quickly identify the methods and actions that are the key features of the role, and utilise them to effect. The 'Behaviours to be avoided' section exists as a guide to limit the excesses of the role, and act as a blueprint for individuals to develop each of the roles into a positive force, especially where someone has a very strong tendency to that role. As we have discussed before, a weakness is very often the over-use of a strength.

To develop a back-up role, take steps to identify and limit the 'Behaviours to be avoided' of your main preference, and practise using the 'Behaviours to be cultivated' of the back-up role. Keep the objective of the new role in mind, and take every opportunity to practice the new behaviours in the team.

A supportive environment in the team will help develop new behaviours. As individual role development is in the interests of team development, the leader and team should be open with their objectives and actions. If they are not open then other team members cannot assist in the coaching and counselling effort and may be confused by the behavioural change.

The notes can also be used to encourage a style or role that needs to be adopted for a different situation, time, or stage of a project. For instance, as an individual development project, try developing the effective behaviours of a Finisher on a Friday afternoon. You will find that you soon develop the ability to tie up the loose ends of work started during the week and enjoy the weekend, free from worry about things left unfinished.

Coordinator

Role objective

To control and organise the activities of the team, making best use of the resources available.

Behaviours to be cultivated

- Encouraging people to achieve the team's objectives by helping individuals to identify their own role and contribution, encouraging them to put personal objectives into second place and providing them with positive and supportive feedback.
- Smoothing over disagreements and unproductive competition by using tact, insight and firm control.
- Identifying weakness in the team balance, and expanding her or his role to compensate.
- Keeping people's efforts oriented in the direction of the team goals, and co-ordinating the use of resources.
- Exercising personal self-discipline in acting as a focal point for team effort, especially when the going gets tough.
- Delegating in a proper and appropriate way.

Behaviours to be avoided

- Rigidity and obstinacy posing as grit and determination.
- Not recognising ability and merit in the team, and not using all possible team resources.
- Refusing to admit superior ability in other team members, and competing with others, particularly Creators and Evaluators.
- Abdicating role in the face of powerful competition.

Driver

Role objective

To give shape and form to the team activities

Behaviours to be cultivated

- Directing the team's attention to the need to set clear objectives and priorities.
- Taking a wide perspective of the team's purpose, and helping members to perceive their own role and contribution.
- Exerting a directive influence on team discussions, and using summaries to set out the outcomes in terms of objectives and targets.
- Giving the team activities an appropriate shape or pattern by co-ordinating the various contributions.
- Keeping a constant, objective and detached view of the team's progress and achievements, intervening only when they are deviating from the appropriate path.
- Intervening when another member is exerting too much influence with an inappropriate idea or suggestion which is in danger of moving the team away from its brief.

Behaviours to be avoided

- Using her or his own role for personal advantage, at the expense of team objectives.
- Using a directive style that assumes undue authority
- Being too intrusive in making summaries, appraisals or interventions.
- Displaying lack of tact.
- Becoming isolated or aloof from the team and losing identity as an integral team member.
- Competing with other team members, particularly Creators and Evaluators.

Creator

Role objective

To act as the prime source of ideas and innovation for the team.

Behaviours to be cultivated

- Concentrating attention on basic strategies and major issues.
- Formulating new ideas relevant to the team's objectives.
- Looking for possible breaks in approach to problems with which the team has been confronted for some time.
- Presenting proposals at times which assist their positive reception.

Behaviours to be avoided

- Attempting to exhibit her or his capabilities over too wide a field.
- Devoting efforts and creative capabilities along the lines of personal interest rather than team needs.
- Taking offence when her or his ideas are evaluated and possibly rejected, making no further contribution to the team effort.
- Being too inhibited about putting ideas forward when confronted by a dominant, extrovert or over-critical group.

97

Evaluator

Role objective

To analyse ideas and suggestions both from within and from outside the team and to evaluate their feasibility and practical value in terms of the team objectives.

Behaviours to be cultivated

- Using her or his critical thinking ability constructively in the team's interests.
- Achieving a blend of experimenting outlook and critical appraisal.
- Building on colleagues' suggestions, helping to develop others' ideas to relevant and practical fruition.
- Making firm but tactical cases against adopting unsound approaches to problems, and choosing the right timing for these.
- Developing a close working relationship with the creative members of the team, especially Creators.

Behaviours to be avoided

- Using her or his own critical thinking ability for personal advantage, at the expense of team objectives.
- Tactless and destructive criticism of colleagues' suggestions.
- Negative thinking – allowing critical powers to outweigh open minded receptivity to new ideas.
- Competitive behaviours, particularly with Coordinators or Creators.
- Lowering team morale by being too critical, or evaluating at inappropriate moments.

Implementer

Role objective

To translate general concepts and plans into a practical working brief, and to carry out that brief in a systematic fashion.

Behaviours to be cultivated

- Helping ensure that the team's tasks have been structured and that the objectives are clearly outlined.
- Sorting out the practical details from the broad brief, and attending to them.
- Maintaining a steady, systematic approach whatever the pressures, or lack of pressure.
- Persevering in the face of difficulty and striving to meet targets.
- Providing practical support and back-up to other team members.

Behaviours to be avoided

- Destructive criticism of team members' ideas and suggestions.
- Lack of flexibility. An Implementer is best when striking a balance between perseverance and adaptability.
- Competing for status within the team by letting her or his strong sense of personal identity get in the way.
- Being too eager to carry out plans before they have been fully developed.

- Over-critical comment on others' ideas for lack of practical application.

Communicator

Role objective

To help individual members to achieve and maintain team effectiveness.

Behaviours to be cultivated

- Observing the actions of other team members, and their strengths and weaknesses
- Supporting team members in their strengths, building on their positive actions
- Underpinning the shortcomings in other team members by personal assistance or by finding appropriate alternative resources.
- Improving communications between members.
- Fostering a sense of team spirit be setting an example and modelling effective team member behaviour.

99

Behaviours to be avoided

- Competing for status or dominance in the team.
- Siding with one member against another or others.
- Conspicuous or pretentious behaviour in the role.
- Letting good feelings get in the way of task completion.

Investigator

Role objective

To explore outside resources and develop contacts that may be useful to the team.

Behaviours to be cultivated

- Using of ability to get on with people to extend the range of the team's contacts and useful friendships.

- Using her or his interest in new ideas and methods to explore possibilities outside the immediate working environment, and introducing them to the team.
- Act as point of contact with outside bodies, keeping up to date with all developments that may be relevant to the team's work.
- Assisting in maintaining good relationships and harmony within the team, encouraging others to make best use of their talents, especially when in times of pressure and crisis.

Behaviours to be avoided

- Getting too involved in her or his own ideas at the expense of exploring others.
- Filtering and rejecting ideas or information before submitting them to the team for evaluation.

- Relaxing too much when the pressure of work eases.
- Allowing her or his liking for talking and sociability to lead to an unproductive use of time.

Finisher

Role objective

To ensure that all the team's efforts are as near perfect as possible and that nothing is overlooked.

Behaviours to be cultivated

- Keeping an eye open for mistakes, especially those that may fall between the responsibilities of two people.
- Choosing areas of work where finishing qualities are important.
- Looking for mistakes in detail that may spoil the finished product.
- Actively searching for aspects of the work which need a more than usual degree of attention.
- Constantly endeavouring to raise the standard of all the team's activities.
- Maintaining a sense of urgency and time-keeping within the team.

Behaviours to be avoided

- Unnecessary emphasis on detail at the expense of the overall plan and direction.
- Negative thinking or destructive criticism.
- Lowering team morale by excessive worrying.
- Reluctance to delegate and involve others in the detailed work.

Tools and techniques

In this chapter there are some ideas that will help you to develop your own personal skills, and the skills of your staff to balance your decision making and problem solving approach. However, if you are in the position of not being able to balance the team on individual grounds, as in the Beta case example, or you want to supplement the changes, you may need to consider using a specific technique or tool to assist in balancing the process. Chapters 14, 15 and 16 contain some examples of the tools available for use in teams or as an individual in each of the stages of problem solving. It is by no means an exhaustive listing, and there are many other techniques available that are appropriate and useful. Some of the techniques are more useful in a team environment, some in an individual situation, some apply equally to both. The table at the start of each chapter will help you to determine the most appropriate tool for the particular situation that you are facing.

A technique does not replace the need for the valuing the stage of the process by yourself or your team. If the team members do not see the need for creative input to the decision making process, then the use of a technique like brainstorming will be worthless. The team will not enter into full participation, will subvert the process and prove conclusively that there is no need for the stage in the decision making process. So it is important that the first step is getting the team to accept the need for the phase – the technique can then help to correct the imbalance in the preferred way of working. In effect, the whole team takes the responsibility for filling the gap rather than relying on the efforts of a specific individual role.

The skills appropriate to each stage

Ready skills – 'Let's imagine it!'

Ways you can help

- Acting as primary source of creativity, imagination, and ideas.
- Providing approaches that are original rather than conventional.
- Ignoring the obvious and focusing on possibilities.
- Finding information and resources from outside the group.
- Recognising new opportunities for the group.
- Proposing how to take advantage of new opportunities.
- Building up contacts outside the group.
- Constantly looking for new ideas and possibilities.
- Supporting the ideas of others.

Ways you can hinder

- Getting carried away with impossibilities rather than just possibilities.
- Spending time on your own ideas rather than paying attention to what the group is doing.
- Trying to solve the problem all on your own rather than with the group.
- Taking offence when your ideas are evaluated or even rejected.
- Getting inhibited about putting your ideas forward when confronted by dominant or critical group members.
- Involving yourself in your own ideas rather than those of others on the group.
- Filtering and rejecting ideas or information before submitting them to the group for evaluation.
- Looking bored when other are not talking about things that interest you.

Aim Skills – 'Let's evaluate it!'

Ways you can help

- Instinctively following through on plans.

- Finishing any task that you begin.
- Preventing careless mistakes from spoiling the success of a project.
- Putting your full attention to a task.
- Providing the only role that applies critical judgement to the group's work.
- Providing reasoned arguments for optional approaches.
- Assessing different options without bias or prejudice.
- Analysing situations for all the possible problems and opportunities.
- Staying cool under pressure and continuing to think straight.

Ways you can hinder

- Emphasising details at the expense of the overall plan.
- Criticising those who have unusual ideas.
- Lowering group morale by worrying about time and details.
- Not involving others in the detailed work.
- Focusing on the urgent rather than the important.
- Using your own critical-thinking ability for personal advantage at the expense of the group objectives.
- Tactless and destructive criticising of suggestions by others.
- Thinking negatively rather than thinking critically and thus preferring conventional to original approaches.
- Competing with other team members.
- Lowering group morale by being too critical or evaluative at an inappropriate moment.
- Staying objective at a time when the rest of the group is getting enthusiastic.

Fire skills – 'Let's do it!'

Ways you can help

- Keeping the focus on the objective.
- Coordinating the activities of the various group members.
- Involving everyone in the task.
- Recognising talented people in the group and get them working on the objective.

- Driving to achieve results.
- Challenging inertia, ineffectiveness or complacency.
- Attacking time wasting activity.
- Challenging a majority view.
- Organising and planning action steps.
- Using practical common sense.
- Willing to work hard.
- Providing clear sense of reality and feasibility.
- Understanding and using systems.

Ways you can hinder

- Disguising your rigidity and obstinacy as grit and determination.
- Listening too long to someone whose point of view has not been heard.
- Asking people to do things that you could do yourself.
- Refusing to admit superior ability in other group members and compete with others, particularly the Creator and the Evaluator.
- Abdicating your role in the face of powerful competition.
- Using your own role for personal advantage, at the expense of group objectives.
- Assuming undue authority.
- Becoming too intrusive in summarising, appraising or intervening.
- Acting tactlessly.
- Acting aloof from the group and not acting as a group member.
- Competing with other group members, particularly the Creator and Evaluator.
- Destructive criticising of others ideas and suggestions.
- Persevering on a task that no longer needs to be done.
- Competing for status within the group.
- Carrying out plans before they have been fully developed.
- Criticising others for their lack of practical common sense.
- Criticising others for talking about things rather than doing things.

Summary

Your preference for one stage or another in the problem-solving process can be balanced in one of several ways. You can balance the team by taking on secondary roles. You can balance the team by importing the skills you lack from outside. You can balance the team by using a technique to overcome the gap. You can assist in balancing the process by being aware of the gap in the need and being supportive of others in their attempts to provide the necessary back-up. The team role counselling notes assist in developing a back-up role or refining one's own preferred roles. The answer is to share your differences and value the other perspectives; look for synergy and spend time refining your own preferences and secondary roles.

105

10

Ready – Aim – Fire and quality management

Quality management or its more evocative title Total Quality Management (TQM) is one of the supertanker trends of the 1990s. A supertanker has a momentum that is difficult to stop – you need to start slowing down a supertanker about 20 to 30 miles from the port in order to dock safely. TQM has developed a pace and momentum during the 1980s and 1990s to the extent that if you are not pursuing a programme, you are in the minority of businesses, and likely to go out of business soon (according to the TQM pundits and gurus). Most supertankers are also Japanese built and operated. The Japanese have eclipsed the ship building and operating companies of other countries, and every year's Fortune Global 500 and Fortune Global Service 500[1] shows the Japanese domination of most industrial and service sectors – they have the largest banks, the largest trading companies, the largest electronics companies, the largest steel companies. The Japanese are the world's greatest exponents of TQM, and their ability to continuously improve their operations means that they will probably stay leaders – they have a 20-year start on most Western firms.

TQM is therefore something that you cannot ignore. But many people are put off by the jargon and the confusion of the conflicting systems and processes sold by the main consultancies. They each peddle their own 'right way' that has its set of directives and imperatives, and its own problem solving approach. What would help is some standardisation of approach and style that applied the best processes in a single language. This would make implementation easier and facilitate the culture change necessary for successful continuous improvement. Can the Ready – Aim – Fire process provide that single approach?

---

[1] *Fortune* magazine publishes annual reviews of the 500 most successful and largest industrial and service companies in the world, analysed by sector

What is TQM?

Total Quality Management is a process that focuses the organisation strategies, objectives and action on to customer needs and aims to deliver the product or service that the customer wants, on time, every time. Rather than inspect for defects, TQM looks at improving the process in order to prevent defective work. To do this TQM aims to involve everyone in the organisation in the quality improvement process, seeking opportunities for continuous improvement in their area of work.

Most TQM programmes have these three elements in common – customer focus, process improvement and involvement of people. They often differ in their techniques and implementation styles. Many of the generic programmes often ignore or pay lip-service to the different needs of the client organisation. At the other extreme, organisations that have tried to implement their own programmes without any external guidance have misled themselves into believing their own hype. Both extremes – the one approach that applies to all situations and the home-grown approach that does not reflect an objective viewpoint – do not achieve the results that are expected. In a survey of why this happens, a lack of internal integration of the TQM process with the rest of the managerial activity is found to be one of the major reasons.[2] Successful TQM implementation seems to follow a pattern where a simple, systematic approach is customised to fit the precise needs and culture of the operating organisation.

Ready – Aim – Fire is a simple, systematic approach that fits the needs of the TQM processes. It is a process that bases problem solving and decision making on information not on opinion. It is a process that fosters involvement. It is a process that can be easily defined to be customer focused through the parameters of the Ready and Aim steps. It is a problem solving approach that is ideally suited to process improvement.

Case study: Implementation of TQM using Ready – Aim – Fire.

A major multinational organisation in the electronics industry wanted to introduce a quality management process to its European operations. The driving forces in this strategic decision were:

■ The adoption at corporate headquarters of a formal quality management approach for its world-wide organisation as the prime focus to maintain a competitive advantage.

[2] Jonathan Smilansky 'Why TQM so often goes wrong', *Crossborder,* Summer 1993

- The need to assimilate new acquisitions and organisations into the culture of the parent company in a rapidly expanding marketplace.

One of the major concerns of the company's senior management was that any process that was introduced needed to be flexible enough to accommodate different approaches and speeds of development in the different countries, departments and companies that made up the total organisation. It would not be an imposed way of working that was standard across the organisation, and it was not to be bureaucratic and centralised. It would be decentralised with the individual management teams taking ownership of the pace and style of development in their own area, consistent with the general organisation direction.

The management committee first set out a broad plan that followed the Ready – Aim – Fire approach to launch the initiative. They would spend some time gathering information for themselves on the quality process and the needs of their organisation before developing vision and mission statements for the organisation to provide the strategic direction and launching the full involvement of the workforce.

108

They went out collecting information and ideas in the Ready stage. They called in consultants to help them with awareness training and conducting surveys of customer needs. They visited other companies who had already implemented a TQM system and learned some of the positive features and the pitfalls. They participated in a number of workshops where they stepped outside of the consideration of existing information and ideas and created possible scenarios and innovative ideas for their organisation environment. At the end of a full six month period of immersion in the concepts and ideas of quality and customer service, they were ready to move to the next step – Aim.

Over a sequence of three workshops, each lasting one day, they pulled together the information that they had gathered and put it into some priority order for analysis. They ranked the customer information, the information from employees and the information from other organisations and weighed the results against the innovative and creative ideas that they had developed. They formulated a vision and mission for the organisation that would act as the direction finder for the different countries and departments in their own development process. The management committee also set themselves some strategic objectives that they would be responsible for, focusing on two or three of the major areas for improvement that were identified in their analysis sessions.

Having decided on what action to take, the committee then moved its focus to implementing that strategy – they moved to Fire. An action plan was drawn up for each of the strategic goals with people and time resources allocated and agreed. A major management conference brought together the whole of the European management team for the first time under one roof, and the whole process was launched, transferring the responsibility from design and direction – the management responsibility – to involving everyone in the process. Regular review points and milestones were set so that progress could be checked and corrected.

The management committee had followed a Ready – Aim – Fire process in their overall decision and implementation of the initiative. It was now the turn of each of the individual country and departmental managements to carry out the same process in their own organisations. At their Ready stage there was the need to collect relevant data on their particular situation – they looked particularly at the internal customer relationships and worked in the overall umbrella of the organisation vision. Using the Ready – Aim – Fire process for their decision making, they each developed their own vision and mission and set of priority strategic goals that were aligned to the total organisation direction.

There were a number of very striking differences in emphasis that developed at this step. Some newly acquired companies had already followed a TQM approach, and they managed to set very challenging targets and goals for some very specific improvement projects. At the other extreme, a number of operations in Eastern Europe realised that they would have to set their priority in the education of the staff in the concept of quality and participative decision making, and it would be several months, if not years, before they could develop the same level of improvement project as their colleagues.

The process is flexible enough to allow greatly differing speeds of implementation and a range of different priorities all aligned to the direction of the corporate mission. There was no imposition of a specific timetable or rigid system of quality. There was no mass training of all staff. Instead, each manager took responsibility for her or his areas and identified their own priorities and action plans using the Ready – Aim – Fire approach. An upward cascade of priorities and direction ensured that the direction was consistent and aligned, and that the local developments did not detract from the overall plan.

Improvement teams were set up in two main areas – functional improvement and cross-functional improvement. As their agreed process for problem solving they used Ready – Aim – Fire. The teams took time at their initial meetings to ensure that they had a good balance and that they knew the techniques necessary to supplement and support their problem solving. The training in problem solving methods and team work was carried out using the real life improvement project as the learning medium rather than the more removed atmosphere of the classroom case study and exercise. Thus the staff were trained and improvement achieved simultaneously.

As the individual departments and countries achieved their goals, so they looked at their benchmarks and collected more and more relevant data, and continued to set new strategies and implementation plans. The Ready – Aim – Fire process became a cycle where one implementation plan was collecting more data for the Ready stage of the next improvement project.

The organisation has made a number of significant improvements in its first two years of using the process. The ability to operate at different speeds and in different cultural environments with success has meant that the local staff have learned the concepts and direction with greater ease that might have been the case with a more rigid, imposed structure. The ability to mould and build on the local culture has allowed for greater ownership of the process as 'theirs' not a programme handed down from Head Office. The continued development of centres of excellence inside the organisation has also allowed for internal benchmarking for the slower developing units, and has provided a ready source of facilitators and trainers for the project teams. It is often easy to submerge the enthusiastic and achieving groups under a cloak of standardisation and adherence to a single-pace implantation plan.

Overall, the implementation has been a success, and the Ready – Aim – Fire process has been widely used and acclaimed by participants for its ease of use, the flexibility to be used on several different levels and applications and its acceptability.

110

Ready – Aim – Fire and customer focus

This is one of the major focus points of a TQM process. By using the Ready – Aim – Fire approach to your dealings with both internal and external customers the information gathered will be more accurate that it is at present. At best most of us will guess what the customer wants and then try to sell them our solution to their assumed needs, rather than listening openly to their own statement of need. As Tom Peters says 'Listening is not telling the customer how good your product or service is!' [3]

Being aware of our own problem solving preferences, we can approach our conversations with customers and suppliers in a more open way, being sure that we collect information and data on the true nature of the issue (Ready) before making decisions and taking action (Aim – Fire). We will get more accurate data on our customers' needs and thus be able to satisfy them (and even delight them) more often.

The case of the customer need

Basil is a senior sales director in the tax and duty free division of a multinational

[3] Tom Peters, *A Passion for Excellence* video, Video Pubishing House

FMCG company. He thought he knew what his customers wanted. Working with his management team, he put his 25 years of experience to work and quickly came up with the clear message that the one item that affected customer sales and the one thing that his customers valued above all else was price. The lower the price, the more he could sell to the retailers in the duty free shops and airlines. The higher the price relative to their competitors, the less the retail customers would stock, and his company's products would be less available to the consumer.

In the light of the need for accurate data for planning a new organisation strategy, Basil agreed to go and ask one or two of his most important customers for confirmation. (A sceptical consultant working on a quality initiative in the company had managed to place sufficient doubt in his mind that price might not be the only factor for him to want to gather the proof that he was right.) With each customer visit, the style and the outcome was the same. Basil was greeted as a friend – there is not a great deal of staff turnover in this specialist part of the business, and if people do move, they often move to another company and keep their same customer contacts. Many of his buyer contacts were personal friends and golfing partners as well as being business colleagues. Basil was careful to put a lot of time into building the personal relationship as he knew that was important in the price negotiation.

Due to the friendship, Basil could be direct: What makes you buy from us in preference to our competitors? The answer was equally direct for each buyer: 'Three things – price, price and price!' Basil had his confirmation that the consultant was wrong and his 25 years of experience were right. But to check he probed a little: 'OK, I know that price is important, but what do you really value when it comes down to the really important decisions like the size of display area you will put up in the shop and the range of brands you stock? What differentiates us from our competitors – is it just price?'

Basil waited for confirmation of what he knew to be true – if he sold at a lower margin, then he would get more shelf space. As a result he nearly missed hearing the answer: 'What we really value is the speed that you put right any problems that we have in deliveries and stocking. We have unpredictable surges of demand, and your logistics people are excellent at finding spare cases of product for us at short notice so that we can keep the shelves stocked. That is really important to us. We also appreciate the personal contact and friendliness of everyone in your company, not just you. People we have never met treat us courteously and with a genuine desire to be of service. That is important. And we have confidence in your determination to help us in every way possible – your merchandisers work hard to understand what we want and then do it, your logistics people often call us about orders when there is a change to the pattern to check that we have it right. Yes, price is important as it affects our margins, but I will tell you in confidence – don't use this against me next month – your price is higher than both of your major competitors, and yet we give you more shelf space. We are much more confident of your ability to satisfy all of our other needs for continuity of supply and problem solving – these are more important to us.' A similar response came from every one of the customers that Basil talked to about their needs.

At the next sales meeting with his team Basil reported back on his meetings and admitted that in his 25 years he had been doing all of his planning and decision making on the wrong assumption that price was the most important buying factor. Having now discovered the other customer needs were more important, he needed to change his teams' whole planning approach and actions to ensure their current excellent reputation was maintained and enhanced. Instead of looking for further cost reductions, he put effort in building internal relationships with logistics and accounts to reduce the number of errors in internal communications and thus give a better service. By balancing his preference for the Fire stage (as many in a sales and FMCG environment have) with a determined effort in information collection and avoiding prejudicial assumptions, Basil had now defined the issue, and could Aim more effectively.

112

Ready – Aim – Fire and process improvement

The second major cornerstone of TQM is the focus on process improvement. How we do something is as important, and sometimes more important, than what we do. The aim of most organisations is to get their people doing the right things right. But mistakes and errors happen, and our immediate assumption is that someone made a mistake – they did the right thing wrong. We focus our attention on the small number but visible problems and miss the greater number, and more damaging invisible problems where people are doing the wrong things right. They carry out processes and procedures that are hopelessly out of date, or out of step with the current needs of the organisation, but do them very well. In surveys in organisations, between 60 and 80 per cent of the waste in organisations is estimated to be due to people doing wrong things right.

The case of the filing system

Liz is the secretary and assistant to the Human Resources Manager of a major multinational. One evening, her new manager brought the whole team together to blitz the personnel file archives. In the course of the evening work they threw out and destroyed almost 90 per cent of the files, filling 62 industrial waste sacks. They threw out copies of candidate application forms and rejection letters that went back over ten years or more. They found files of correspondence on management conferences and training courses long since past, some of which were cancelled. They destroyed tons of duplicated information.

At the end of the evening they had created a space in the office where four people could sit and with a value of over £20,000. But the biggest shock was yet to come. Liz explained that she was about to start a major project that had been set as one of her objectives by the previous Human Resources Manager. She was about to start to microfilm the entire archive. As Liz was a very conscientious and dependable worker, she would have done it very well. She would have done it right, but she would have been doing the wrong thing. The new manager had prevented a very costly exercise in doing the wrong things right.

The Ready – Aim – Fire approach in process improvement helps to prevent the wrong things being done by giving people a systematic way of questioning every action. The Ready stage looks for old and new ideas – not just the way we have always done it, but why do we do it at all? What is the customer need? Is there a better way? The Ready stage gathers new ideas to blend with the old ideas and allow for a clear analysis of the current situation and a decision based on fact not opinion, before going into an implementation stage. Process improvement teams, or individuals looking at what they do on a regular basis will find that Ready – Aim – Fire, and the use of some of the techniques outlined in Chapters 14, 15 and 16 will give a systematic problem solving and process improvement process that can be applied to any situation. Liz was prevented doing the wrong thing right by a lucky change of manager. The rest of us should not trust to luck, we should question everything and look for continuous improvement.

Ready – Aim – Fire and involvement of people

Company-wide quality improvement will not happen without the involvement of people. Employing more checks and inspectors will increase the quality of the product and service getting to the customer, but at greater cost. The only way to reduce errors and reduce costs at the same time is to prevent the errors occurring in the first place. This means getting everyone to own the quality of their output and to look for ways of making improvements. If you do start to involve everyone in the process, they need access to a problem solving approach that they can quickly and easily learn and use that can be applied to most situations.

Ready – Aim – Fire is an easily understood approach, and can be introduced with varying degrees of complexity and sophistication depending on the needs of the people concerned. Once armed with a way of dealing with situations, and some back-up techniques, staff develop the confidence to ask questions and to make improvements, and get more involved in the process. Ready – Aim – Fire is therefore very useful at the individual level.

Much of the involvement of people in quality improvement is through their participation in problem solving teams, looking at improvements that fall outside the immediate individual sphere of responsibility. In problem solving teams, the Ready – Aim – Fire approach is very effective both with the overall problem solving process but also with the team development opportunity through the sharing of preferred roles and achieving a balanced approach.

114

Summary

Ready – Aim – Fire is ideally suited to the quality improvement process. It can be used for broad strategic direction setting and for the identification and solving of individual problems. It helps to develop the involvement of people by giving a easily understood process and by helping to develop teamwork and sharing of information. There is no confusion over using different models and terminology for different situations. Being a very flexible process, it also avoids the pitfalls of the predictive and more structured quality systems that demand that the whole organisation is treated as a standard unit.

11

Ready – Aim – Fire and change management

'We live in turbulent times.'

'The only certainty is that there is no certainty.'

'Change is that period of uncertainty between two changes.'

'Continuous change is the norm of the nineties.'

'Keeping pace with the rate of change is the secret of success.'

All of the above statements have been made about the times we live in and the absolute importance of coming to terms with the rapidly changing business and social environment in which we operate. Some books try to identify the trends so that we can use them to help our planning. As John Naisbitt, author of the best-selling book *Megatrends*, puts it 'Trends, like horses, are easier to ride in the direction they are already going.'[1] Understanding and managing change and confusion is an absolute essential for any successful business in the 1990s. What is the key to successful management of change? John Naisbitt again: 'The most reliable way to anticipate the future is by understanding the present.'

Change management starts by getting a clear understanding of the present, getting a clear idea of the future and then setting a path between the two. Ready (collect data on the current situation), Aim (create a vision of the future situation), Fire (draw up an action plan to bridge the gap).

In the above diagram the change management process is shown with the Ready – Aim – Fire equivalents. Interestingly, while the stages of Ready, Aim and Fire are followed in the correct systematic order, when

[1] John Naisbitt, *Megatrends – Ten Directions Transforming our Lives,* Macdonald & Co, 1982

Fig. 11.1 Ready – Aim – Fire and the change process

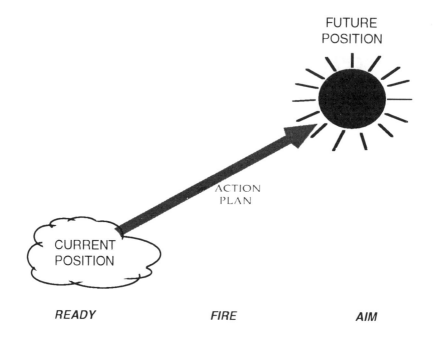

you draw the process as a diagram they appear as Ready – Fire – Aim. This apparent problem can be used in group discussion to discuss constructively the importance of carrying out the analysis of the change process in the correct order and the danger of missing out one of the stages.

Ready – Where are we now?

If you don't know where you are, then there is little likelihood of knowing where you are going, and less chance of deciding how to get there. Knowing your current position is an essential step in navigation, and if you are trying to navigate your organisation or yourself through the turbulent waters of the global environment, you equally need to know where you are now to make any sense of the rest of the information. The Ready stage in managing change is all about collecting information on the current situation. Depending on the nature of the organisation and the seriousness of the situation, the data needed will be different, but data are needed to have the right base for the next steps.

Information needs to be gathered on what the current position is for the organisation. What are the financial numbers? What are the communication issues? What do different members of staff think? What is the opinion of customers? What do suppliers think? What is the current business environment? What have been the recent movements in the environment? What is the political and legal framework? What are the social and economic trends at the present time? What are the current problems facing the industry? the company? the department? the team? the family? me? What are their priorities? What general patterns emerge from this information?

All of these questions and more are relevant to building a picture of the current situation. To collect information from within the organisation, beyond the documents and records, focus groups and surveys are often the most useful instruments and focused workshops are very helpful in prioritising and making sense of the information gathered. Focus groups and benchmarking will give information from outside the company, plus detailed analysis of competitors.

In gathering information at the Ready stage it is important to recognise the tensions and stresses that there will be among people who favour the Aim or Fire stage, or have a bias towards judgemental decision making. There is always a tendency to assume and make quick assessments, often due to the pressing need to respond to the situation. But, just like navigating a ship or aircraft, an imprecise measurement or an assumption made in haste can cause you to end up miles off course, to lose your way, or even worse to crash. So there is an absolute need, if the change pathway is to be understood and analysed correctly, for there to be an accurate Ready stage – a balance of factual and opinion data, of logical and relationship information. In other words, the emphasis of the stage is to balance the Sensing and Intuiting and Thinking and Feeling preferences in the organisation – to gather as much information as needed to obtain a whole and holistic view of the current situation.

What information is relevant, and how much is required will depend on the scale and complexity of the situation, but there is an old adage that you can never have too much information – that is almost certainly true when you are dealing with the plethora of influences that bear upon most situations. There is always a tendency to move on too quickly, and miss a vital clue or piece of data. At the other extreme, we must avoid paralysis of analysis, where the means becomes and end in itself. We can easily put off a decision by immersing ourselves in the data collection process, never feeling that it is time to move on.

That is why the next step is closely linked to the Ready stage – Aim.

117

Aim – Developing the future

As the current situation is analysed and the priorities and trends are isolated, so a future direction will start to emerge. In the change management process, one moves from considering the current situation to identifying the future. What is our desired outcome? What is the vision of our organisation in the next five years? What are the potential scenarios for the future? How do we see ourselves in ten years' time?

By focusing on the future situation that we are trying to create, we identify a vision of where we want to be. This vision of the future give us our direction, our aim, our mission. In organisations, a clear vision can engender enthusiasm and bring together the disparate parts of the organisation into one co-ordinated effort as described in the main case study in chapter 10. In that multinational example, the widely different needs and aspirations of the different departments, companies and nationalities were all brought together to work towards a single vision of the future. Each of them developed their own vision and mission, but they were aligned to the overall direction of the group.

Fig. 11.2 Examples of an aligned organisation and a non-aligned organisation

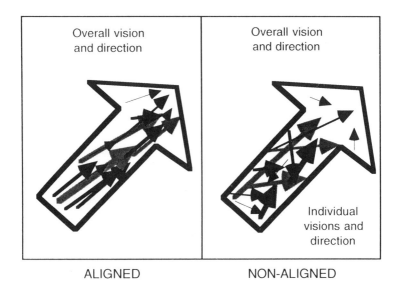

ALIGNED   NON-ALIGNED

The aligned organisation brings together everyone's individual vision into a consistent pattern and direction. The individual arrows are all different, showing the difference between the speed and depth of the action of the component parts, but they are all pointing in the same direction. In the non-aligned organisation, the chaos of all of the individual visions is clear. In reality, the clash of the action plans of the individuals and groups associated with that form of organisation will mean an incredible waste of energy and resources in fighting battles against each other. In the aligned organisation, the energy is conserved and can be directed to fighting the competition.

When developing a vision statement, it must be clear and understandable to all personnel, at all levels of the organisation. It needs to be brief enough for most people to remember and yet reflect the competency of the organisation and its strategic thrust. The vision should be broad enough to allow flexibility in implementation but not so broad as to permit a lack of focus; it should serve as a template and be the means by which managers and others in the company can make decisions. The vision must reflect the values, beliefs and philosophy of the company and reflect the organisational culture. Whilst it should be worded so as to generate enthusiasm, it should not be unrealistic which could make it a source of derision. A good vision is a balance between stretching and attainable goals.

119

Once the vision and mission of the organisation is clear, the gap is established between where we are and where we want to be. The transition steps of the implementation plan can then be plotted in the Fire stage.

Fire – Making it happen

The Fire stage in change management is all about putting strategies, goals and action plans together to take the necessary action to achieve the vision. Once the direction is clear, then the action plans are often easy to create. Action plans that are formulated from an analysis of the current position alone will generate progress but to a destination that is unknown and may be totally wrong once achieved. If the vision is stated in a clear and precise way, the steps necessary and the priority issues become clear. If the vision is more general, there may be several possible implementation plans to achieve the end result.

For example, a specific vision of achieving success through teamwork and empowerment suggests an immediate focus on developing team relationships and delegating responsibility, flattening organisation structures and developing people oriented policies. A vision that only talks of increasing shareholder wealth may have the same action plan which would have a positive long-term effect on the profitability of the company, but could also suggest an action plan developed for the shorter term that is focused on reducing costs, selling off assets and reducing overheads.

The vision sets the goals. The implementation plan sets the strategies and objectives. A matrix can be drawn up to link the strategies to the goals and make sure that the intended plans will impact the goals. In this way any goals that are not met by the strategies and plans can be clearly identified, as can those areas where too many strategies are focused on one goal, possibly causing conflict or over-emphasis. In either case, the evaluation of the implementation plan can be made at the planning stage when it is easy to develop corrective action to the plans. Measures and milestones can also be developed so that the implementation plan stays on track.

120

Table 11.1

EXAMPLE OF A GOAL AND STRATEGY ALIGNMENT MATRIX

	GOALS			
Strategy	Empower employees	Customer satisfaction	Shareholder return	Teamwork
Training in quality and service	●	○	○	○
Establish project structure	○			●
Open new markets			●	
Improve communications	○			○

● Strong correlation   ○ Weak correlation

Table 11.1 above shows a correlation between strategies and vision goals. In this example the gap is clearly visible in meeting the goal of customer satisfaction. The management team will need to consider establishing a strategy more closely directed to achieving this goal if the overall vision is to be reached.

The case of the competitive pressure

The board of directors was facing some difficult economic facts. The level of return was reducing, the market was not growing and a competitor had just released a new product that was rapidly taking market share away from their traditional stronghold. They were being forced to make some major changes or they were facing the possibility of going out of business.

The board met in crisis session. They analysed their current situation – the strengths and weaknesses, opportunities and threats. Each director had run a focus group session with the departmental staff before the meeting to pull together the employees current feelings and analysis of the situation. A consultant helped to pull together the threads of a picture of the problems.

They had a good product range in the motor accessories market, but there had been no real development work done on the main-selling product for a number of years. This was now under attack by their competitor who had developed a computerised control system that surpassed their hydraulic model. The competitive product was more expensive, and was showing some teething troubles, but it had more functionality and greater flexibility. There was no doubt that it would be a real threat to the core business within the next two years.

A concern relayed through the staff focus groups and the customer surveys was linked to this loss of market position.There had been little product development in the preceding three years, and the image of the company was one that was solid, but old fashioned. It had a reputation for good workmanship but no design flair. Internally, costs of manufacture had continued on a steady rise as working practices had not been reviewed and production machinery had a poor maintenance record. Customers were generally loyal and praised the attentiveness of the company; deliveries were always on time, invoices were accurate and the products were very reliable.

A bigger problem was the financial community and the shareholders. The returns and dividend had been falling steadily over the past five years, and the borrowing had increased to cover marketing deficits. The banks and investment houses were demanding a radical improvement. So, the current situation was summarised by the Managing Director as being grave but not terminal. There were sufficient strengths to build on, and the staff were expressing their feelings of concern and accepted the need for some changes.

The next stage – Aim – needed the board to switch their focus to their dreams – what they wanted the organisation to feel like in three to five years' time. After brainstorming and discussing some of the important values for the future, they agreed a draft statement that they would discuss with some key staff and customer focus groups before refining and agreeing a final document. Their draft stated: 'Within five years we will be the supplier of choice in all of our major markets, delivering increased returns to our shareholders through reducing costs, product innovation, customer service and employee involvement.'

The staff groups reacted strongly to the main focus, as they saw it, of the shareholder interests over those of the employees and customers. Although the board had meant there to be a balance of the three interests in their statement, they were convinced that the returns would come through the innovation and involvement, so they revised their final statement to reverse the position of employees, customers and shareholders. The final vision was: 'Within five years we will establish ourselves as the supplier of choice in all of our major markets, through customer service, employee involvement, product innovation, and profit generation thereby delivering increased returns to all our stakeholders.'

Comparing the current position and the vision, the board then identified five major strategic focus items for the immediate future. They would institute a total quality management process to focus on customer service and improvement groups to reduce waste and to maximise the profitability of the current product lines. They would set up a development programme that would redesign their complete range of products over a three year cycle. Thirdly, they would reorganise their management structure to project teams integrating the complete process flow of a product line. They set up a communication improvement programme to keep everyone involved and informed on the measures of progress. Finally, they planned a major cost reduction exercise in the inventory of raw materials and finished goods through a just-in-time warehousing system.

Plotting these strategies against the goals of the vision, they felt that the goals were well covered, with the exception of the shareholder return. The immediate impact on profit would be the extent to which the cost reductions could be made through the TQM improvements and the just-in-time system. The other strategies were longer term. They felt confident that they were on the right track, so they put their priority weight behind these two strategies, and set stretching targets and measures on these items. A regular review process was set up, and the whole plan launched to staff through a departmental communication exercise which also began the first stage of the implementation of the improved communication strategy.

Within two years, all of the targets for the profit improvement through the cost reduction programme were exceeded. The employee involvement through the reorganisation into process teams and total quality management generated so many new ideas and improvements to the existing product lines that the pressure on the new developments lessened. The customer needs were being met through the increased functionality on the old models with a reducing price keeping a margin over the competitive products. They exceeded their vision target by two years. However, the board had foreseen that they would achieve their target early and, not wishing to lose the momentum that had been generated, they had convened a cross-functional team to review the direction and focus of the company and develop a new vision that would take them towards the millennium and beyond.

Summary

Using the Ready – Aim – Fire approach for change management follows the process of establishing the current position – where we are now, then the desired future position – where we want to be, and then the implementation strategies and plan – how do we get there. It is important to follow that sequence to ensure that you end up where you want to be or try to implement strategies and plans that are not based in reality.

123

12

Ready – Aim – Fire and project management

What is project management?

A project is a set of activities, linked together over a period of time, which are carried out to produce a specific goal or goals. Using this definition, you can easily see that project management applies to more than the traditional engineering and construction contracts where the terminology is most used. Projects can still be large scale like the development of a new oil field, the building a new factory, or the design and development of a new car. These projects involve hundreds of people with varied specialist skills working together to meet the overall goal. They may take years to complete at a cost of millions of pounds.

But projects can also be small scale, involving no more than a small group of people, often working on the project for only a short period of time. These projects have outcomes like producing an in-company newsletter, organising a meeting or conference, arranging a golf outing, redecorating a house. Whilst the scale and content of these projects may be vastly different, there are some key processes and skills that are common to all. These skills and processes are often linked together under the title 'Project Management' and have been closely guarded by the professional engineers and project management specialists as their personal domain and source of power. The project management processes and tools are in practice relatively simple and systematic approaches to ensure that the planning and scheduling of the project is effective. The same processes and tools that are used in the construction of an oil refinery can be used to construct a new factory, build a new house or install a new bathroom. Only the scale and complexity changes.

Whatever the size of the project each member of the project team (or an individual if it is an individual project) must possess technical and personal skills to complete the project on time, to specification and within budget. The technical skills are the task skills associated with the discipline of the individual – engineering, market research, human resources, construction, design – and are determined by the context and subject of the project. Personal skills include management of the activities of the project and communication with team members and clients – these are common attributes needed across all disciplines.

Project management and Ready – Aim – Fire

Each project, whether large or small moves through a cycle of phases. There is a need to identify the client needs and the scope of the project. The aim is to produce a project definition that focuses on what the project is designed to accomplish and why it is being undertaken. In the overall management of the project this is the Ready stage – collecting the data and information from the client and making sure that you have sufficient information to proceed to the next stage.

125

Aiming a project means analysing the various alternative strategies for achieving the project and checking the feasibility of the chosen strategy. This defines how the project is to be implemented. Once a strategy has been agreed with the client, the project moves on to the Fire stage of planning and implementing the strategy.

The Fire stage then involves producing plans to achieve the quality, time and cost parameters of the project; establishing a completion sequence; analysing potential problem areas and developing a people plan to carry out the project. This clarifies what is to be done in task detail, who is responsible for each task and by when it will be completed. The project then moves on to the action stage of implementation – controlling the work in progress; resolving differences and maintaining the schedule with the aim of delivering the project output to the client. Eventually, on completion, the final step in Fire is to evaluate the success of the project, review what has been learned and what can be applied to future projects.

Just like in using Ready – Aim – Fire in quality management, the problem solving cycle can be employed within each stage to ensure the effective completion of that stage. So very often to complete the Ready stage of a project you will need to go through one or more complete Ready – Aim – Fire cycles to determine various factors and features. As the project grows in complexity, so the number of stacked processes will increase.

Table 12.1

PROJECT MANAGEMENT TASKS AT EACH STAGE

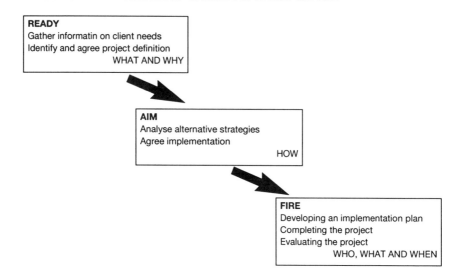

Fig. 12.1 The Ready – Aim – Fire cycle

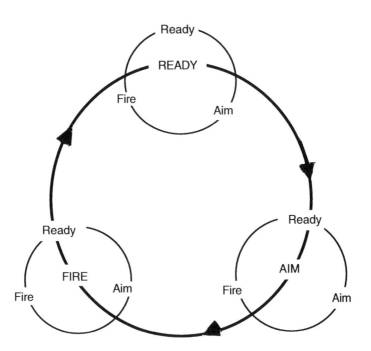

Project management tools

Many of the tools and techniques included in Chapter 16 are those closely associated with project management. They are used during the Fire stage to assist in the planning of the most complex or the most simple of projects. Most are to be found on the many computer software programmes that are available to assist in the compilation and drawing of the scheduling and planning diagrams. The work breakdown is the basic step in planning. It breaks down the total project into individual sections and eventually into specific tasks and responsibilities. Once a work breakdown has been made, the information can be used to create the two most common project management tools, the bar chart and critical path analysis, both of which show the relationship between each task and the time allotted.

The bar chart plots the tasks against time, and allows you to view the resources necessary and the status of the project at any given time. It is often referred to as the Gantt chart after its originator, and full details of how to construct and use one can be found in Chapter 16.

127

Critical path analysis focuses on the dependency of one task on another. A project is by definition a set of activities or tasks that are linked together to achieve a goal. Very often you cannot start one task without completing another. For example, you cannot start to build the roof of a house until you have completed the walls, and these cannot be started until you have dug the foundations. There is therefore a critical relationship between these three tasks, and the length of the project will be determined by the total time spent on following this critical path through the tasks. Many other tasks can be completed at the same time and will not affect the critical path. For example, work on the interior of the house can be done simultaneously with the completion of the roof tiling; the plumbing and electrics can be installed at the same time. Critical path analysis helps you to determine which of the tasks need to be closely supervised and completed on time if the final delivery date is to be met. Again, full details of critical path analysis are to be found in Chapter 16.

Implementing projects

Implementing is a process of balancing the three main project objectives – cost, time and performance. Just as making good decisions requires a balanced process like Ready – Aim – Fire, Implementing the project requires continual reference to this balance and making changes as the client's needs demand. Thus the client may be willing to compromise a little on the original performance specification in return for an earlier delivery or lower cost.

Fig. 12.2 The project triangle

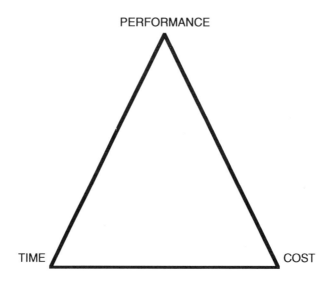

Project management checklists

READY
- Discuss project with client.
- Draw up a project definition.
- Agree project definition and objective with client.
- List and agree project outcomes.

AIM
- Brainstorm alternative strategies.
- Evaluate alternatives.
- Choose strategy and agree with client.

FIRE
- Break down project into steps.
- Determine performance standards for each step.
- Define time needed to complete each step.
- Determine sequence of steps and critical path.

- Define total time needed and timetable.
- Determine cost of each step and total budget.
- Agree standards, costs and time with client.
- Design staff organisation and responsibilities.
- Determine what training is required for staff.
- Develop policies and procedures for control.
- Carry out a Potential Problem Analysis.
- Monitor implementation progress against standards, time and costs.
- Take corrective action where necessary.
- Keep client informed of progress.
- Deliver final product or service as specified and agreed.
- Evaluate success of final product or service delivered.
- Carry out review of project.
- Summarise successes and problems encountered.
- Give feedback on personal performance to staff.
- Carry out final audit of project and final reports.
- Publish the points learned in order to benefit other projects.
- Agree close of project with client.

The case of the office move

Jenny was given the task of organising the move of her office from one part of London to another. Her client was the Managing Director of the firm who wished to consolidate all of the firm's London operations under one roof to save on travel time and cost in moving between offices and to improve communications between the individual groups. The numbers of people involved were not great – three people regularly worked in the office that was to close. Neither was the distance great – a matter of a couple of miles, so there was little, if any, disruption to the staff concerned. Managing the project would not involve handling too many personal problems and issues, it would be a matter of co-ordinating all of the different tasks to make the move smooth and keep the customer service continuous.

The first task was to agree the definition and scope of the project with the Managing Director – the client. Jenny arranged a meeting to discuss the parameters. What exactly is required? By when does the move have to take place? Is she to manage merely the physical move of the existing office, or is she to oversee the conversion work on the new site? Why is the move taking place? What are the cost constraints? What, if any, are the limitations due to technology needs?

129

Jenny tried to get a very clear picture of the definition of the project so that both she and the client knew what was expected. They agreed that the project was to organise the logistics and removal of the office to the new location by the end of the third quarter within a budget limit of £40,000 and with no break of service to the customers, both external and internal. The project was not to include the lease discussions and construction plans at the new location. These would be handled directly by the Managing Director, who was already present on site.

Jenny had completed the Ready stage of the project. She knew exactly what her client expected from her and she knew the parameters within which she was to work. The most difficult task that she could immediately foresee was to ensure that everything was completed on time whilst still doing her other job. There was precious little time available to devote to any new project, so she would need to be well organised.

She began to think about what alternative execution options were available to her. She could do everything herself. She could see whether there was someone in the new location to whom she could sub-contract the work, like the person who manages the new office construction. She could bring in an outside agency to manage the project. She could try to get other agencies to take on responsibility for their own specialist activities and co-ordinate them herself. She analysed the options, and discussed them with a colleague in the office who was far better at evaluation and analytical thinking. Jenny's preference was for action, so she knew that she needed to balance her inclination to get on with the job with someone who could make sure that she was doing the right thing.

After talking the options through with Pat, they both felt that the best use of Jenny's time and the best way to ensure that the project was completed to a high level of technical quality was to take the final option. Jenny would work with some of their current service suppliers where there was a high degree of technical input, for example: the computer cable trunking, telephones and fax systems, office furniture and filing storage. There was an opportunity to package parts of the project to these specialists to handle all of the requirements and ensure that the new installations contained the best equipment for the current and future needs. Jenny would co-ordinate these efforts and manage the project. As she was still concerned that she would miss some items of importance with the pressure of her current job and her tendency to Fire – Fire – Fire, Pat suggested that she purchase some computer software that would help with the control of the project.

Armed with her plans about the organisation of the project, Jenny convened a meeting with the Managing Director, her client, to discuss and agree the approach. He was delighted with the analysis and the idea. One concern he had was the liaison between the new office construction and the move. There was a critical timing between the two, that a number of items would need to be planned and ordered well in advance to ensure the move took place on time, but there could be delays in the construction and lease negotiations. Jenny felt sure that with the computer programme to help with some of these critical links that she would have sufficient prompts to discuss progress at the new site that this could be accommodated.

So, Jenny then moved on to her favourite phase – getting things done. The first step was not too easy, as she had to plan the project work breakdown and the critical path, but the computer software helped her by giving prompts and making the construction of the critical relationships easy. She even started to give the computer some 'what if?' questions to check out the feasibility and effects of some different plans. That allowed her to develop the optimal plan where she programmed the computer to remind her on critical points in the process. This would allow her to get on with the rest of her work without worrying about whether something needed to be done on the project.

Meetings with the sub-contractors were easy, as she had planned their inputs and her requirements in detail. They were to be totally responsible for their part of the project, advising on the needs, purchasing and installing the equipment where necessary and ensuring that on NO-Day (New Office Day) everything was operational and switched over. The contractors appreciated the freedom to get on and do what they are best at doing without interference. Jenny appreciated the ability to hand over the responsibility for a lot of the details to other people and get on with her other work.

Using the computer-designed Gantt charts and critical path analysis as a guide, Jenny agreed a review point with each of the contractors some days, or even weeks, in advance of the critical timing points to discuss progress, depending on the nature of the contract and the lead times necessary for that equipment or service. These were programmed into her diary schedules and reminders linked to the project planning charts on her office wall.

In final implementation, the construction was delayed by several weeks due to difficulties with the leaseholder. Because Jenny had managed to link her timetable to that of the construction completion date, she was able to move her schedule easily to accommodate this. Moving quickly round the Ready – Aim – Fire cycle to deal with each problem, she worked with the engineers and suppliers concerned to gather information on the current position, analyse the options available and take a decision on the best way forward, then implementing that plan. As a result, many orders for equipment were delayed and engineers re-deployed without any penalty. These cost savings alone more than justified the purchase of the planning software. Jenny felt able to take overall control of each situation, and most times she briefed the Managing Director on the outcome before he had heard from the construction manager that there had been a difficulty.

Summary

For the office move project, the use of the Ready – Aim – Fire approach was a success, especially as Jenny recognised that she needed help to balance her own potential to leap into action too quickly. The overall project was planned and executed to perfection, and the issues that occurred during the project that often throw things out of line were handled by using a Ready – Aim – Fire problem solving sequence. Ready – Aim – Fire can be applied to any size of project and allows the project manager to have a systematic process that works towards success, and gives the project client the confidence that everything is under control.

13

Ready – Aim – Fire and career management

Are career ladders disappearing?

A major report from the Institute of Management[1] in 1993 looked at trends in management careers over 13 years from 1980 to 1992. Their key findings in that report found that managers are now changing their jobs more often. The direction of these job moves is changing: managers are moving sideways or downwards more often and moving upward less often. Managers are changing jobs for their own personal choice less often and are more often subject to job changes imposed by their employer. The 1992 recession period in Europe has had a marked effect on increasing the number and regularity of job changes.

The report goes on to point out some of these differences in detail, for example in 1980–82 (a previous recession) 66 per cent of managers in the sample changed jobs for the purpose of career progression, promotion, or some other personally motivated, proactive reason. This percentage who were moving for personal, proactive reasons in 1992 had fallen to 43 per cent.

In contrast, the reactive changes of job due to the imposition of a change by the employer through redundancy, transfer, dismissal, or restructuring accounted for only 21 per cent of moves in 1980-82 but had risen to 41 per cent of moves in 1992. The most significant rise came from organisation restructuring, rising from 8 per cent in 1980-82 to 25 per cent in 1992.

[1] Professor Kerr Inkson and Trudy Coe, *Are Career Ladders Disappearing?*, Institute of Management, 1993

Up is not the only way

The report concludes that whilst it is not possible to determine whether the effects identified stem directly from the recession or reflect longer term structural change, the message for managers is that their future career scenario will be markedly different from the 'onward and upward' tradition. Managers will need increasingly to take ownership of their own career, and in particular of their own portfolio of skills. They will need above all to be prepared for change and to seize it as an opportunity rather than view it as a threat.

Beverly Kaye has long argued that career development does not have to equal promotion.[2] In her book *Up Is Not The Only Way* she identifies five directions for personal career development:

UP — traditional promotion.

ACROSS — sideways or lateral development, getting breadth of experience and developing different interests.

IN — developing a more specialist position in the same function, going for depth of knowledge and expertise rather than for breadth of knowledge and experience.

DOWN — moving downwards in the organisation to take, perhaps, a less stressful position and use one's expertise for other activities, such as mentoring.

OUT — moving to another position outside the current organisation.

Each of these directions is a development option and a career path, though many of them (especially ACROSS and DOWN) have been tainted by the view in our traditional hierarchical organisation cultures that they meant side-tracking or demotion. The Institute of Management report, mentioned earlier, and many career management writers and researchers support the view that managers need the skills to make these wider choices of career development and there is therefore a need to change the attitude of individuals and organisations towards career development.

Taking control

To succeed in the 1990s and beyond, managers must take ownership of their own careers. Without their own hand on the tiller, their ship will

[2] Beverly Kaye, *Up Is Not The Only Way,* Prentice Hall, 1982

134

spend a long time off course, following the winds of change that blow through organisations and industries and they will either end up at a destination that they did not want or floating aimlessly in the doldrums, unable to move further for the lack of a breeze in any direction. Many organisations have begun inviting more individual input into the corporate structures of succession planning and career development. Managers need the skills to make these decisions and build their own futures, while organisations need to be more flexible in their planning.

If all of the work on developing career paths is done by individual managers, then they will become increasingly frustrated with the inflexibility of the organisations that they work for, favouring those who can offer flexibility and an employment contract that recognises their individual aspirations. On the other hand, if the organisation changes without encouraging individuals to develop their skills, then chaos ensues. So the effective approach must be a balanced one – a well-organised and simultaneous development of the individual skills and the organisational structures.

135

Ready – Aim – Fire and career management

For both individuals and organisations, the process can be covered by the same Ready – Aim – Fire process. At the Ready stage, you gather all of the relevant information. To Aim, you look to the future environments and make some decisions about your direction (in a similar way to using Ready – Aim – Fire for change management), and in Fire, you implement plans and steps to meet your goals. The difference between individuals and organisations is one of scale and focus. Let us first consider the process applied to individual development:

The case of Jim Bolton

Jim was working as a senior nurse at one of London's busiest hospitals. He had been a nurse ever since leaving college and had progressed steadily up the nursing profession, gaining specialist experience in a number of departments. He saw the nursing profession as a career, and naturally expected to continue to rise up the ladder through promotions that would come automatically as his experience and qualifications increased.

Then, about three years ago, Jim started to feel less than happy with his job. He was married and had two young children with whom he enjoyed spending time. Unfortunately, his shift working and the long hours involved with nursing work meant that this valuable personal time was disrupted. He often worked on weekends and evenings, thus missing the only times that his children were now at home, as they had both started at primary school and were out of the house all of the day. These worries were beginning to affect his work and he felt that he needed to change. He went to see his nursing manager.

Jim's manager, Kate, listened to Jim's problems and his proposed solution. Jim felt that he was now at the stage where he could expect a promotion to a more senior position that would bring with it a transfer on to day working. Kate reviewed the career history and the needs of the organisation and concluded that there was no real opportunity to meet with Jim's request within the next three to five years. The staffing levels were being reduced overall, and many of the more senior positions were being eliminated to reduce the bureaucracy and hierarchies that existed before the hospital became an NHS Trust. Jim was distraught. His only way of getting more time with his children had been eliminated.

Luckily, Kate had some experience of career counselling and knew that there were several other possibilities available that might accommodate Jim's need for more quality time with his children, but they needed some decisions to be made about what Jim really wanted to do. He had never before considered any career or life plan, the job had provided all of the options, and he just went along with them. Kate realised that Jim would need some help. She introduced him the Ready – Aim – Fire process for making career and life decisions.

She drew two rough circles on a piece of paper. It looked a little like a fried egg! She pointed out that the larger area, depicted by the white of the egg was all of the skills and opportunities that existed for Jim. They only stopped spreading all over the page by the constraints and limits that were on the outside. The yolk of the egg represented all of the demands that were limiting Jim from the inside. The white of the egg therefore represented the degree of choice that existed for Jim.

If they could draw the pattern for Jim, with some detail, they would amass all of the possibilities that existed that Jim's skills and potential allowed him to do, within the constraints of the demands he made, like being at home for more of the time with his family. Kate explained that most of us tend to limit our choice by assuming that there are too many constraints on us and too many demands being made. We often even invent extra demands and constraints so that we do not have to make a choice. We grow the size of the yolk and reduce the area that the egg can spread into so that the white is almost hidden.

Armed with a positive outlook and a process to support him, Jim went off to look at all of his possibilities. He listed all of his skills and did some work thinking about what he really wanted from the rest of his life and career. He looked at the different ways of developing himself, and talked things through with his partner and several other friends and colleagues. He completed the Ready stage and went back to have another discussion with Kate.

Fig. 13.1 Amount of choice available

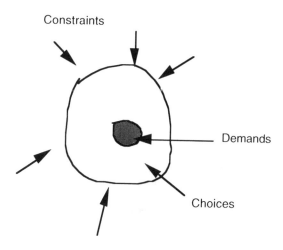

Fig. 13.2 Limiting the choice available

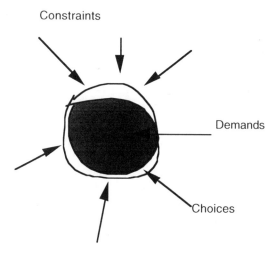

This time Kate moved on to helping Jim to Aim. She got him to consider what was going to make the difference for him. He had recognised that his skills did not limit him to nursing as a career or to the one hospital or even to this country. He had the ability to do other things as well by applying his skills in other areas. But the choice was too great. Kate helped to narrow the choice by dreaming about his ideal future.

Jim realised that he did not want promotion as the last two jobs that he had taken on had caused him extra stress and were moving him away from his real love which was patient care. He initially rejected moving back to a nursing job as that would be seen as a demotion by his colleagues and he could not afford the drop in salary. Anyway, all nursing jobs were shift work, so there would be no improvement in his time off. Jim envisioned himself working in primary patient care and spending time with his children as they grew up. He would live in the same area but spend longer in the local community where he had many family and social connections that had been neglected over recent years.

Kate helped Jim to narrow down his options by doing some forced ranking with him and by adding some realism to some of the options that Jim had identified. Community care emerged as the best fit. There is a great demand for nurses, especially psychiatric nurses to work in the community. He had some psychiatric training, but it was fairly early in his career. Kate knew of secondment opportunities where Jim could gain the necessary up-to-date experience in a local hospital that was in their Trust Group. They moved to the Fire stage of implementing the plan. The secondment was set up, Jim enrolled on to an evening class to update his qualification and set a target of moving into psychiatric community nursing within the next year. That would give him time to re-adjust his financial commitments to cover the lower pay, and perhaps even set up some other part-time agency nursing work for the odd week-end to supplement the finances. It would still take a year of hard work and time away from the children, but the goal was positive and motivational to make that investment worthwhile.

The case of the nursing manager

Joan was the nursing manager of a group of hospitals. Her problem was to ensure that the group's staffing needs for nursing were met at the lowest cost. She had recently seen an increase in problems of staffing the current situations, let alone the future. Many nurses were leaving the profession, and some of the more specialist positions were left unfilled for long periods, yet there were people who had the skills in the hospitals. There seemed to be a gap between what the hospitals needed and what she could provide. In the short term, the gaps could be covered by contract staff, but that could not go on forever.

Joan looked at the needs that she had and the skills base. She went into an information collection exercise. She found countless numbers of staff who had qualifications that were not properly recorded and accessible to her. She found that many nurses were leaving because they did not find job satisfaction in their current positions and had no one to help them sort out some options. She found a large proportion of de-motivated staff in the current jobs because they were not sure of their own future and the current position did not suit them. There was a general feeling of powerlessness in the hospital at all levels.

Having collected this information, and discussed the situation with some career planning consultants, she identified two main problems. Firstly, she did not have a skill record in the hospital to be able to match the current and developing individual skills with the demands made, current or future. Secondly, the current staff were not provided with the skill or opportunity to develop their own careers, hence their de-motivation and frustration.

Two issues to go into action on – two Fire projects, but with strong connections between the two. She set about offering career development counselling to all of the nursing staff, introducing them to the Ready – Aim – Fire process and how to list all of their possibilities and start to make plans to get control of the rest of their careers. As a result of their own analysis of skills, Joan was able to build up a record base of skills, qualifications and expertise that far exceeded the previous records. Qualifications and skills that had been gained in other jobs, at other hospitals and at evening classes were all added, and very quickly Joan was able to fill jobs from within that she had previously had to go to external agencies to fill. For example, she discovered language skills to allow her to move bi- and tri-lingual nurses to work in wards where there were a large number of non-English speaking patients.

139

At the same time, the discussions that she had with nurses on what the future needs of the profession were enabled them to make choices about their own career goals and take steps towards them. The future needs of the hospital would be mostly met from internal development. The career development discussions and training also allowed staff to come to terms with the new demands being made on them by the changing working and economic environment. No longer would they wait to fill 'dead men's shoes', they would be proactive and work on the new information available. The level of frustration and feelings of being powerless in nurses changed to one of motivation and empowerment. The organisation and the individual benefited from sharing the responsibility for career development.

Inplacement and outplacement

Reactive moves doubled in the 1992 recession over the previous recession. By contrast to the above case studies, redundancy and reorganisation often lead a company to make its first contribution to the career development of its managers – outplacement. Outplacement is undoubtedly successful and it is a real benefit to those made redundant. But what about those who are left behind in the newly reorganised company in which they are supposed to do more work with fewer people?

And what about the possibility of career development for everyone before reorganisation and redundancy. As can be seen from both the organisation and individual perspectives of Joan and Jim, it is better to have an 'inplacement' service that helps people whilst they can still add value to the company. Both parties gain.

A goal is a dream taken seriously

The essence of career planning is summed up by the phrase 'A goal is a dream taken seriously', first coined by my colleague Walt Hopkins, and the central feature of his work on life and career designing.[3] Without a dream you have no direction, you have no control over your career path. You just let things happen. But it is not enough to just dream as nothing will happen until you take that dream seriously. You put an action plan together and start with the first step. You collect your information on skills (Ready) you create your dream, your vision of where and what you want to do (Aim) and you set up an action plan to achieve it (Fire). Our files are full of examples and case studies where seemingly impossible dreams have been achieved by the simple step of making a start and believing that it can be achieved.

Summary

The Ready – Aim – Fire process introduces practical steps that enable both individuals and organisations to increase the number of options and to choose the most appropriate option in career planning. It allows and encourages organisations to develop a database of organisational resources and opportunities that can be matched with each individual's database of skills and goals to determine the potential for both the individual and the organisation. It allows and encourages individuals to take control of their own career path and identify the options and directions that motivate them so that these can be discussed with organisations to meet a match with their needs. Working together, both individuals and organisations make better use of skills, set clearer goals, and reach those goals more quickly.

[3] Walt Hopkins, *A Goal is a Dream Taken Seriously*, Organisation Design & Development, 1986

14

Developing 'Ready' skills and techniques

In Chapter 9, there are some ideas that will help you to develop your own personal skills, and the skills of your staff to balance your decision making and problem solving approach. However, if you find yourself in a situation where this is more difficult than normal – for instance, if the team has an overwhelming bias towards one of the stages of Ready, Aim, Fire – then you may need to consider using a specific technique or tool to assist in balancing the process. The following three chapters contain some examples of the tools available for use in teams or as an individual in each of the stages of problem solving. It is by no means an exhaustive listing, and there are many other techniques available that are appropriate and useful. Some of the techniques are more useful in a team environment, some in an individual situation, some apply equally to both. The table at the start of each chapter will help you to determine the most appropriate tool for the particular situation that you are facing.

A technique does not replace the need for evaluating the stage of the process by yourself or your team. If the team members do not see the need for creative input to the decision making process, then the use of a technique like brainstorming will be worthless. The team will not enter into full participation, will subvert the process and prove conclusively that there is no need for the stage in the decision making process. So it is important that the first step is getting the team to accept the need for the phase – the technique can then help to correct the imbalance in the preferred way of working. In effect, the whole team takes the responsibility for filling the gap rather than relying on the efforts of a specific individual role.

The Ready phase of the process is concerned with collecting information about the problem and generating alternatives and possible solutions. The data collection techniques involve sampling, surveys, using checklists and gathering information. Creating possible solutions and alternatives come from the use of a number of creative techniques such as brainstorming, morphological analysis, making collages and lateral thinking.

Table 14.1

'READY' TOOLS AND TECHNQUES

	Data collection	Generating alternatives	Individual	Team
IMPACT ANALYSIS	●			●
BRAINSTORMING		●	●	●
INNOVATION DIALOGUE		●	●	
COLLAGE		●		●
BE THE PROBLEM		●	●	●
METAPHORS AND ANALOGIES	●	●	●	●
MORPHOLOGICAL CONNECTIONS		●	●	●
WHY? – WHY?	●		●	●
SIX SERVING-MEN	●		●	●
DATA BASE	●		●	●
SAMPLES, SURVEYS, CHECK SHEETS	●		●	●

Impact analysis

Where problems are difficult to define, Impact analysis can be used. Unless situations and issues are properly stated problem solving techniques do not work effectively.

The process works by assembling a group of people who are affected by the situation, issue or problem under consideration and asking them to describe, in as specific terms as possible, the impact of the current situation on themselves and others. The major points in the individual stories are summarised and recorded on a flipchart and the common features and major differences highlighted. Through discussion, a consensus of the real scope of the problem can be made.

Brainstorming

Brainstorming is one of the most frequently used techniques in creative problem solving and can be used on its own as a freewheeling activity to generate the maximum number of ideas on a given topic, or as part of another technique such as Fishbone Diagrams where the brainstorming is much more controlled and focused. It is a particularly useful technique to use to inject energy and fun into a group activity, and to break down the traditional barriers to creativity.

Probably due to its popularity, brainstorming is one of the most misused creative thinking techniques. Very often 'brainstorming' is used by team leaders to create a sham of participation and sell their predetermined solution to the team. Even when teams or individuals use brainstorming with the right intentions, there is a tendency to leap to judgement on the ideas too quickly, thus missing a vital incubation step. Brainstorming is designed to be fun and freewheeling, but it uses a structured process to ensure that it is successful. There are a set of rules for the group to follow, and a clearly designed procedure for the whole activity.

143

The rules are designed to aid the creative thinking process, and overcome some of the blocks to developing new ideas that are inherent in everyone. By suspending judgement and criticism these barriers can be overcome, and the creative potential of the group released. The rules are:

- **No Criticism**
  Any idea that is put forward is valid. The group members must not pass judgement or criticise any ideas in the idea generation phase. Judgement must be suspended until the ideas evaluation phase.

- **Freewheeling**
  Each person should be free to contribute an idea at any time, and build on others ideas as well as coming up with their own. As a starter, to get the process going, it is sometimes advisable to do one or two idea collection rounds around the table, with each person contributing an idea before throwing the process open to freewheeling contributions. This beaks the ice and ensures that everyone gets to contribute at least one or two ideas.

■ **Quantity not quality**

The idea is to generate as many ideas as possible. Brainstorming is about quantity not quality in the first instance. Set a target of say 100 ideas in 20 minutes.

■ **Record every idea**

Every single idea must be written down, however crazy, and even if it is the same as a previous idea stated in a different way. This reinforces the freewheeling possibilities of piggy-backing an idea on to a previous one. This often sparks off further new ideas or applications.

■ **Incubate before evaluating**

This step is the one most often missed out by groups. The group should stop after the ideas generation phase, and take a actual break, in some cases overnight or longer. This break allows the ideas to incubate in individuals' brains, often generating new connections and feasibility not obvious in the first evaluation.

Table 14.2

THE RULES OF BRAINSTORMING
No criticism
Freewheeling
Quantity not quality
Record every idea
Incubate BEFORE evaluating

To carry out a brainstorming session, you will need at least one flipchart and plenty of flipchart paper and pens. (White-boards are not suitable for brainstorming as they do not have a large enough surface area to write on. The electronic copy boards that produce a photocopy of the ideas recorded on the surface can be used, so long as more than one is available. If there is only one copy board, the delay in recording ideas while the surface is printed and cleaned will interrupt the free-wheeling nature of the brainstorming session.)

Once you have set up the necessary equipment, introduce or restate the rules (see Table 14.2 above) and post them up on the wall so that everyone in the group can see them. Next, write up the subject at the top of the flipchart. What is to be brainstormed? Using wording like 'How many' or 'How to' in the subject statement will help to direct the group to generating ideas and solutions.

Someone has to be appointed to record the ideas on the flipchart. The main requirement is for someone who can write quickly and legibly. There are two other considerations in choosing a scribe:

■ The person wielding the pen is in a very strong position in guiding the process. She or he can have a profound effect on the outcome and progress of a brainstorming session by re-wording people's contributions or filtering ideas. You must have someone who will write up exactly what is said without question or comment.

■ The scribe will be very busy concentrating on listening to the contributions and writing them on the flipchart. This means that they will not be able to contribute many ideas themselves. You therefore do not want to handicap your most creative person by using them in this role.

To get the ideas flowing, it is best to give participants a few seconds to think and jot down one or two ideas themselves, then go around the table collecting one or two ideas from each team member. Record all the ideas on flip charts, even if they are restatements of a previous suggestion in different words. It is very important that there is no discussion or criticism of the ideas at this stage, nor any comment made on them. Criticism or early evaluation inhibits people from contribution. When a flip-chart page is full, have it pinned up around the wall so that you have the ideas in view all of the time. It is a good idea to use more than one flip-chart so that the scribe can continue to write down ideas while someone else pins the completed sheet up on the wall. Let the session continue until no more ideas are being generated or the time limit is reached.

145

If it is planned to continue immediately with the evaluation phase, take a break and limit the immediate discussion to questions of clarification of the ideas, not criticism. If possible take a longer break, say overnight, as this will allow for more reflection and association to take place. Keep the lists in view during the incubation period and let the members silently take in the full range of ideas and options generated.

As pointed out earlier, one of the difficulties in managing the brainstorming process correctly is to stop premature evaluation of the ideas. Very often groups or individuals will pick on one idea and proclaim it to be the best without giving due consideration to the others. To overcome this tendency, the following process should be followed. Before eliminating any ideas as impractical, get the group to review each of the ideas as follows: Which ideas are positive? Which ideas can be grouped with other similar ones? Which ideas are not positive but interesting? Mark the positive reactions on the charts, and if necessary rewrite the ideas to allow the grouping process to be effective. The purpose of identifying interesting ideas is to use them as further springboards to develop options. Only after these three steps have been taken should any ideas be crossed off the lists as impractical. The pared-down list then gives you a small number of potential and interesting ideas for further analysis and consideration.

If you are using brainstorming as an individual activity, you will find it useful to work in short bursts of activity, no more than three to five minutes at a time. During the periods in between the idea creation phases, your brain will continue to work on the problem and process ideas in the subconscious. Often these will flash into the conscious brain without warning, so it is a good idea to keep a pencil and paper handy to record these at any time (especially at the side of the bed to record ideas that occur during the night!).

Innovation dialogue

This is an activity that is conducted in pairs, and provides a very quick and powerful way of developing an innovative solution to a problem. It is therefore very useful if you are working on an individual activity and need to generate some Ready ideas quickly, as you only need to find one other person to work with for a maximum of 15 minutes – the process could even be carried out over the telephone.

Innovation dialogue relies on two elements in the process for its success. First there is a strict time limit on the various steps. This encourages the participants to reduce their descriptions to the essentials, thus avoiding the tendency to persuade each other or to include too much detail in their statements. The second process element is to force the problem owner to consider the positive side of any suggestion first. This overcomes the strong tendency to always consider the objections and negative side first.

To complete an innovation dialogue, one person is the problem owner, seeking a possible solution to a problem that they have, the other person acts as a 'consultant'. Although the term consultant is used, no consultancy skills are necessary for the consultant role – what is required is to follow a process and to give a personal opinion on the problem posed by the problem owner.

By following the process and strict time schedule, the problem owner will develop a solution and implementation plan within 15 minutes. At the end of the dialogue the problem owner has the choice of carrying through the idea developed to implementation or to consider other alternatives.

The first step in the process is for the problem owner to describe the problem and the essential background to their consultant partner. The time-limit for this step is two minutes. During this two minutes you must get across the principal features of the problem so that the consultant can react. The consultant is allowed to ask questions of clarification only.

The second step involves the consultant outlining their immediate thoughts on a possible solution. Again, there is a strict time-limit of two minutes for the consultant to put forward their ideas. During this two minutes the problem owner should listen carefully to the suggestion, taking notes if necessary or desired. She or he should offer no comment or criticism at this stage on the solution or idea given, and any questions are for clarification only.

The third step moves on to the consideration and evaluation of the idea or solution suggested by the consultant. To keep the focus on the positive attributes of the idea, the problem owner must state three positive things about the consultant's suggested solution before any concerns or criticisms may be voiced. These positive features should be shared with the consultant. To further keep the discussion on the possible, any objections should be voiced by using the wording 'How to ...'. For instance, instead of saying 'There is no supporting information' the statement should be 'How to get supporting information?'

147

Once the positive features and criticisms have been shared, the final few minutes should be spent working together to refine the original idea into a workable action and implementation plan.

Collage

Sometimes in the Ready stage, you need to get your team to look at the problem in its totality, or express themselves in a different way in order to tap into the creative possibilities. Collage allows a group to express itself visually, but by using the stimulus of images and words created by others, it avoids the need for the group or individuals to have any artistic ability. Collage works particularly well where a group cannot express itself adequately in words, and therefore needs some stimulation. It is therefore particularly useful to allow a group to express feelings, and views of the future, so it is particularly useful for groups that do not have a balance of Feeling preferences.

If you plan to use this activity at a team meeting, you need to do some preparatory work. You will need to gather together a large supply of magazines and newspapers, ensuring that there is a wide range of different publications to give a range of images and ideas.

First clear a large working area either by joining several tables together or moving the furniture to the side of a room and clearing a large floor space. Tape together a number of flipchart-size pieces of paper to make a base for the group collage whilst still allowing enough free space in the room for members to freely walk around and interact with each other. (Allow up to one piece of flipchart paper for each person.)

Next, explain to the team that the task is to create a picture depicting the problem, issue, situation or environment under consideration (for example: the desired future situation).

With the magazines, newspapers and journals as a resource, everyone in the team takes a selection at random, and searches them for images, headlines, pictures, words, cartoons, etc. to which they are attracted in the context of the situation they are trying to describe. At the start of the process individuals should work on their own rather than discussing within the group, collecting a pile of cuttings on the subject from their own perspective. When each person has collected a number of cuttings then they can start to create a group collage by sticking them on to the background paper. Now there will be more discussion with colleagues and a group understanding of the problem will develop, along with some innovative insights into the issue.

Once the collage is complete, allow the group time to look at it in detail, and discuss the meanings of the various parts and the whole with each other. At this time the overview given by the collage can help to draw out themes or observations that are important to the problem, issue or situation under consideration.

As a variation to the group exercise, each individual in the group creates her or his own personal picture. Give out one sheet of flipchart paper to each individual, and then encourage each person to complete their own collage independently of others in the group. Then have each person explain their own collage in a 'Show and Tell' before joining the group in a discussion of the overall points being made, drawing out the observations and themes important to the issue or situation. This variation allows individuals to show their own feelings first, before trying to build them together into a team understanding and viewpoint.

A further variation of this exercise is to have individuals or a team draw a picture without using images from magazines or journals. This obviously requires less preparation time, but does depend a little on the artistic ability of the participants. Those who feel self-conscious about their lack of skill may be inhibited and therefore their contribution may be affected adversely.

Be the problem

Another exercise or activity that uses visualisation to overcome the barriers that some people have in creative thinking is called 'Be the problem'. This activity requires individuals to develop a personal identification with a problem and through that analogy investigate possible solutions. 'Be the problem' can be used to create a better understanding of the nature of a problem and point towards potential solutions. It can also help a group to visualise possibilities that would not otherwise be recognised in a situation. A third use is to work though possible solutions to a problem to compare their effectiveness.

149

In asking individuals to 'Be the problem' they have to stretch their imaginations and not only see the problem but also get right inside the issue, the situation, the machine or whatever and experience it fully. Outcomes from this experience will point the way to understanding the nature and extent of the problem so that it can be better defined. Experiences can also provide the stimulus to creative solutions to complex problems.

Start by identifying the problem or situation to the group and then ask each individual in the group to imagine themselves in the position of being the problem. Allow one or two minutes for people to associate with this (it often helps if people close their eyes and are guided through a looking and imaging the feel, the smell, the sounds, the taste, the view of the problem from the inside).

Then go round the group and ask each person in turn to describe their experience, noting down any important insights. While everyone is still working on their personal analogy, you can even encourage discussion between the group members when they stay in the role of being the problem rather than being outside observers. Whilst still in the role, the group may also find it useful to imagine how they might solve the problem from their current perspective.

To use the same idea to test out alternative solutions, ask one member of the group to 'Be the problem', and for other members to 'Be the solutions'. Each solution can then be tested by the 'Problem'.

Metaphors and analogies

Creative insights can often be generated by comparing the problem to another activity and searching for similarities and differences. In a group or individual activity, creating metaphors can help to develop new insights into a particular problem, and thus develop a greater understanding in the group and possibility of finding solutions. Metaphor can also be used to explain a complicated idea in simple language. Analogies are more appropriate where the problem under analysis is closely linked an item or object rather than an action or activity.

We use metaphors are in everyday life in both of the scenarios for which this activity is designed. Many new ideas have been developed as the result of using metaphors. For instance, it was the comparison of the atom to the solar system that led physicist Niels Bohr to develop his model of nucleus (sun) and electrons (planets). In explaining complex ideas a computer memory is often compared to a tape recorder.

Metaphor and analogy eliminate a common problem solving block by by-passing normal logic conventions and making connections between two dissimilar objects or situations. It is therefore useful to use in situations where you have a strong Sensing, Thinking and Judging bias.

Metaphors and analogies can be generated as an individual exercise, as an individual activity in a group with each person in the group thinking up their own and then sharing them with others, or as a group discussion. In a group situation, the individual thinking step gives everyone in the group an opportunity to contribute an idea. As a group discussion the freedom to build on other people's ideas may be more creative, but this is achieved at the expense of involving everyone.

To find a subject or object with which to compare your problem, either pick an item or activity at random or choose one or more subjects from the list in Figure 14.1 or 14.2. Think of all of the similarities and differences, and note them down. The insights that this process creates will help in the understanding and definition of the problem at hand, and help in determining the data collection requirements.

Morphological connections

This activity can be used to generate large numbers of potential and creative solutions which can then be further evaluated. It will prevent groups and individuals becoming locked into only considering previously known options. This technique can be applied to a number

Fig. 14.1 Metaphor generation list

Riding a horse	Baby-sitting	Sunbathing
Climbing a mountain	Reading a novel	Putting up a tent
Digging the garden	Mixing a cocktail	Putting on make-up
Jogging	Planting seeds	Scoring a goal
Getting married	Writing a book	Fishing
Playing the piano	Flying an aircraft	Watching a film
Using a computer	Selling encyclopedias	Central heating
Cooking a meal	Driving a fast car	Washing dishes
Scuba diving	Taking a dog for a walk	Fighting a battle
Having a bath	Conducting an orchestra	Playing golf
Winning a competition	Sailing a dinghy	
Planning a dinner party	Writing a letter	

Fig. 14.2 Analogy generation list

Car	Chair	Book	Table
Town	Lawn	Horse	Stadium
Flower	Knife	Dog	Fish
Fence	Child	Man	Camera
Woman	Glass	Guitar	Window
Bicycle	Ice cube	Letter	Plate
Drum	Tree	Sand	Computer
Egg	Football boot	Caravan	Photograph
Beach	Sausage		

of situations where there is a requirement to break down the barriers to creative thinking about alternatives. It relies on a forced association between alternative components as defined and generated by the group.

If you are planning to use this technique with a complex problem, a large number of components and alternatives may be generated that will make information handling difficult (4 components with 5 alternatives each will give 625 different combinations). In such cases access to a computer would be helpful to process the information and the activity is best conducted over at least two sessions, and with extra time allowed for the analysis of the database of information.

As an example, suppose we wanted to develop a new form of human transportation. We would first agree a list of the component parameters of the problem. In this case there needs to be at least a means of supporting the traveller and a method of propulsion. Other parameters can be added if appropriate – the larger the number of the parameters of the problem, the greater the number of combinations that will be generated.

Next list the alternative possibilities for each of the parameters. For a means of support there could be a seat, a bed, a sling, a platform to stand on, etc. As a method of propulsion: steam, electricity, gas, internal combustion engine, magnetism, gravity, nuclear, wind, water, etc. Using a matrix, each possible combination is listed, some of these already exist, like seated / internal combustion engine would be a motor car, motorcycle or bus; standing / water would be a surf-board. Others generated in the matrix would not currently exist. Of these latter possibilities, the feasible and interesting alternatives identified for further analysis.

If more than two parameters are analysed, then the matrix becomes more complex, and the use of a computer spreadsheet or database becomes useful.

Why? – Why?

One part of the Ready skill is to create alternatives and creative ideas, to be expansive. This activity focuses on the need in Ready to collect data and information on the problem. The process involves stating a problem and then repeatedly asking the question Why?, until it cannot be answered. At that stage it can be assumed that the group has uncov-

Fig. 14.3 Morphological connections example

	Seat	Bed	Sling	Standing
Water	?	?	?	Surf board
Combustion engine	Car	?	?	?
Wind	Yacht	?	Hang-glider	?
Nuclear	?	?	?	?
Steam	Car	?	?	?
Electricity	?	?	?	?

ered the root causes of the problem, and can then begin to analyse these in terms of importance.

A large amount of information can be gathered in a group session using the Why? – Why? process, so several flipcharts are required to record the information. You may wish to investigate ways of recording the information on a computer in the form of a flow diagram to cope with complex issues.

In the example in Figure 14.4 below, the problem of a photocopier breakdown is being analysed for all of the possible causes. The problem itself is written down on the left hand side of the paper, then the question 'Why?' is repeatedly asked and all of the answers recorded, until no further answers can be given.

As many sheets of paper will be used to record the answers in a flow chart format they should be pinned to a wall to keep the stages in view. (Remember to number each page so that they can be retrieved and worked on in later sessions. These can be typed or stored in a computer if appropriate.)

Once the process (or the team!) is exhausted, allow time to incubate the information, and let the group read through the complete Why? – Why? diagram. Then begin to discuss the relative importance of the causes identified to guide the direction of further investigation in the Ready stage or analysis in the Aim stage.

Fig. 14.4 A Why-Why diagram

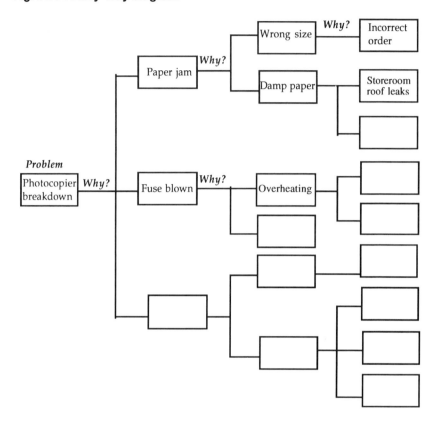

Six serving-men

This is another activity that can be used individually or in a group to help to gather information on a problem, its possible causes and its situation. Six serving men derives its name from the Rudyard Kipling poem which begins:

> I keep six honest serving-men,
> (They taught me all I knew);
> Their names are What and Why and When
> And How and Where and Who.

The analysis of a problem using these six questions as guidance for a brainstorm can often give an insight into the nature of the problem, and where to start further analysis. By asking the same questions about when the problem does not occur will give further dimension to the analysis.

To use the technique, first define the problem as precisely as possible. The more general the statement of the problem, the more general will be the causes identified by the process; so to generate specific causes, a specific problem statement is needed. Then define the individual questions, using the six serving-men as a guide. Each question (What, Why, When, etc.) should be framed twice – once in respect to the problem being analysed (When does the problem occur?), and once in respect of the converse (When does the problem not occur?).

Write each question at the top of a sheet of flipchart paper. Eventually there should be 12 sheets of flipchart paper with a question at the top. These can be posted around the walls of the room and the team asked to brainstorm their ideas in response to each question.

For example, if the problem being analysed is side-impact traffic accidents, the questions could be:

155

- When do side-impact traffic accidents occur?
- When do side-impact traffic accidents not occur?
- How do side-impact traffic accidents happen?
- How do side-impact traffic accidents not happen?
- Where do side-impact traffic accidents happen?
- Where do side-impact traffic accidents not happen?
- What causes side-impact traffic accidents?
- What does not cause side-impact traffic accidents?
- Who causes side-impact traffic accidents?
- Who does not cause side-impact traffic accidents?
- Why are there side-impact traffic accidents in some situations?
- Why are there not side-impact traffic accidents in other situations?

The completed flipcharts will then give an indication of the key issues that require further investigation and data collection.

Database

When you are collecting information in the Ready stage prior to analysis, you often need to organise the data for ease of reference and retrieval. A database is one of the central features of any data collection strategy. It is the point from which all of the data gathering tools are developed, and more importantly, it is the focus of recording that data and information in a standardised format which facilitates further analysis. It therefore deserves careful attention. However, as each project will be different, and the information and data needed will be different, it is not possible to give a template for producing one, though there are several computer programs (d-Base, FileMaker Pro, 4th Dimension to name three of the popular versions) that offer an open framework and guidance on developing the data base.

A data base is a collection of either numbers, words or pictures or any combination of all three. Numbers have an exact meaning and can help in measuring and comparing, for instance: sales volume, man hours, revolutions per minute, material cost. Words are best for describing sequences, decisions, labels, etc. for instance: job descriptions, operating procedures, job cards. Pictures are useful for illustrating relationships, locations, sequences, patterns and sizes, for instance: flowcharts, drawings, photos, videos. The multi-media capability of many computers makes it possible to combine numbers, words and pictures into a single database that can be easily manipulated.

With any computer or manual database, the most important step is to decide what is needed and how it will be recorded. The most elaborate databases may never be used due to the difficulty of inputting the data and the complexity of the analysis process. At the other extreme, too simple a database will not provide the necessary information for effective problem solving. Each database needs to be carefully planned in view of the problem, what is needed, what is available, what accuracy is needed and in what format the data can be collected and stored. There is a very true saying about computer systems that applies equally well to databases: Garbage in – Garbage out.

Samples, surveys and check sheets

There are many ways of collecting information and data, whether or not a database is being used for recording and analysing. When there is a need to collect information from people or to observe the workings of a machine or process, then you may wish to use sampling or survey techniques to reduce the task to a manageable size.

Sampling is a method that is frequently used to get representative information about a problem, when it is not possible to measure the whole population. Because it takes a sample of the population, it is important that the sample is correctly chosen so that the information gathered is valid. There are the three main methods of sampling: random sampling, stratified sampling and systematic sampling.

In random sampling items are picked at random out of the entire population, e.g. names from the employee register, shops from the local delivery plan, items from the production run, etc. This method of sampling is the commonest and often the safest method.

For stratified sampling the population is divided into parts that are different, and each part is then sampled separately using a random technique. So, people might be divided into men, women and children; cars into mini, family saloons, hatchbacks, executive, sports and off-road; and computers by size into PCs, mainframes and minis, or by operating system into Macintosh, MS-DOS. Windows and Unix.

In systematic sampling a sample is taken at a regular interval, e.g. every fourth minute, or every hundred shoppers. This is easier to organise than random sampling, but can be inaccurate unless the items being sampled are randomly mixed.

157

There are some dangerous pitfalls of incorrect sampling – basically the smaller the sample, the less accurate it is going to be. Making decisions based on incorrect or inaccurate data is just as bad as making decisions based on no information. Care should therefore be taken to set up an accurate sample. There is expert guidance available from research consultants and companies, and wherever the population size is large, or the data being gathered is critical to the problem being analysed their advice should be sought.

Surveys ask people their opinions, reactions, knowledge or ideas, and can be based on questionnaires, face to face interviews, or both. They are used to collect usable data about what people know, think or feel about a specific issue.

Planning is the critical stage in conducting a survey to ensure that the information gathered will be valid and usable. As with sampling, designing a survey questionnaire can be a complex operation, and expert advice is available if the data is critical. For instance, questions need to be well designed so as not to lead to a specific response, and also need to be clearly understood and not open to different interpretations.

If you wish to design your own survey, or get your team to design one, then the essential first step is to decide carefully what it is you want to know, and why. The questionnaire needs to be designed for its application – is it planned to be a written test or a set of guide questions for a face-to-face interview? In either event, it should be simple in its wording, so that any misinterpreting is minimised. The design should ensure that answers are concise, as this helps in recording and in collating the data. Some further points to consider would be: in what form are the answers needed? multiple choice? true/false? numbers? range? free form? Each has a specific use depending on the information required. The principle to follow is to let the form follow the function.

When the questionnaire or interview template has been designed, always try out the questionnaire and/or interview with people not involved in the design process, and collate the answers to check the collating system and data base.

Then decide who is being surveyed? Everyone, or a sample? You need to think carefully about who can provide the best information. The questions need to be framed in the language appropriate to the audience, and also reflect the amount of time that the target population can, or will, spare to answer.

When it comes to recording observations, then a check sheet is a valuable tool. A Check sheet is a data recording form which indicates how many times something has happened. It is used to provide a clear record of data gathering, ensuring uniform, comparable information which matches the data base set up for the project.

Fig. 14.5 Example of a check sheet

Number of items in shoppers' baskets at express check-out

Date: 24 June

No. of items	Time						
	0800-0900	0900-1000	1000-1100	1100-1200	1200-1300	1300-1400	1400-1500
Over 13			✓	✓✓	✓✓✓✓ ✓✓✓	✓✓✓✓ ✓✓✓	✓
10–12	✓✓	✓✓✓✓	✓✓✓	✓✓✓✓	✓✓✓✓ ✓✓	✓✓✓✓ ✓✓✓✓	✓✓✓
7–9	✓	✓✓✓✓	✓✓	✓✓✓	✓✓✓✓	✓✓	✓✓✓
4–6	✓✓✓	✓✓	✓✓	✓✓✓	✓✓✓✓ ✓✓✓	✓✓	✓✓✓
1–3	✓✓✓✓ ✓✓✓✓	✓✓✓✓ ✓✓✓✓	✓✓✓✓ ✓✓✓✓	✓✓✓✓ ✓✓	✓✓✓✓ ✓✓✓✓ ✓✓✓✓	✓✓✓✓ ✓✓✓✓ ✓✓	✓✓✓ ✓✓✓ ✓✓✓

Check sheets are usually designed for each data collection task, so it is important to follow a design process. It is also important that the data collected is comparable, i.e. it is homogeneous information – one person, one machine, etc. – otherwise the data will be difficult or impossible to analyse. The purpose of a check sheet is to record 'the number of times' not opinions.

Summary

The techniques in this chapter can be used to supplement the Ready process in an individual or team situation. There are techniques for data collection and for generating alternatives that will ensure that you collect as much information as possible on the problem before trying to agree a solution or strategy. The choice of technique will depend on the situation.

159

15

Developing 'Aim' skills and techniques

The Ready step is all about collecting information and alternatives. It is divergent in its thinking and expansive. The purpose of the Aim step in the problem solving process is to analyse the data and information and decide on the best solution or strategy to implement. The thinking process is therefore convergent and reductionist, evaluating the data and options and agreeing priorities and best solutions.

The tools and techniques that assist in the Aim process are analytical. They will assist you as an individual or your team to determine cause and effect, to prioritise, to evaluate options and to organise the mass of data and options into useful information from which decisions will emerge.

Pareto analysis

Pareto analysis is a process which graphically shows the relative importance of a number of factors. In many problem solving situations, there are a number of potential causes, a number of different situations where the problem occurs, or a number of different solutions to a problem. Often, it is difficult to see the relationship between the different factors, and to isolate the most important issues. Pareto analysis is a technique that helps to focus attention on the 'vital few' factors as opposed to the 'trivial many'. It can be used to identify the cause, situation or idea which has greatest impact.

The process is based on a principle named after Count Vilfredo Pareto, an Italian economist who studied the Italian economy and identified that about 80 per cent of the wealth of the country was held by only 20 per cent of the population. The principle that most of the effect is accounted for by a few of the causes is found to be true in a number

Table 15.1

'AIM' TOOLS AND TECHNIQUES

	Organising data	Evaluating options	Setting priorities	Individual	Team
PARETO ANALYSIS	●	●	●	●	●
PROS AND CONS		●		●	●
CHOICE VOTING		●	●		●
PAIRED RANKING		●		●	●
SELECTION GRID		●	●		●
CLUSTERS	●			●	●
FISHBONE DIAGRAM	●		●	●	●
SWOT ANALYSIS		●		●	●
COST/BENEFIT ANALYSIS		●		●	●
STAKEHOLDER MAPPING	●			●	●
FORCE FIELD ANALYSIS		●	●	●	●
POTENTIAL PROBLEM ANALYSIS		●		●	●

of different situations: 80 per cent of accidents happen to 20 per cent of people; 80 per cent of holidays are taken during 20 per cent of the year; 80 per cent of overtime is worked by 20 per cent of workers; 80 per cent of sales comes from 20 per cent of customers. It is the almost universal application of this 80/20 Rule which is the key to Pareto analysis.

Pareto analysis involves drawing your data into various categories and sorting it into descending order to see if a Pareto pattern exists. The analysis is usually portrayed as a bar graph with the most frequently occurring event at the left, and other events in descending order to the right. Often a cumulative line is also drawn to accentuate the data. For an example of a Pareto analysis chart see Figure 15.1 below.

The chart clearly shows that there are some factors that are more important than others, and generally speaking, more impact will be gained by working on these factors rather than on the smaller impact ones.

Fig. 15.1 A Pareto analysis chart

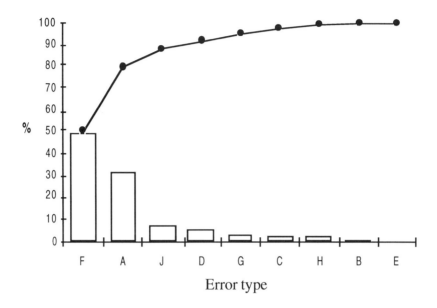

If you are carrying out a Pareto analysis of your data, do not stop at one analysis even if it shows a good pattern. If you repeat the analysis using different categories you will build a complete picture of the problem and in so doing you may identify some issues that are of even more importance. In the example below you can see that a different pattern can be achieved using different categories.

The case of the inaccurate invoices

The accounts section of a manufacturing company had some problems with the accuracy of invoices being despatched to customers. There were a number of different errors, so a problem solving group decided to look for a Pareto pattern in order to focus attention on preventing the most important errors first.

The group chose to collect data on the frequency of errors by type of error, and also the cost of each type of error.

The data collected was as follows:

Table 15.2

	Error type								
	A	B	C	D	E	F	G	H	J
Total errors	41	1	3	6	0	65	4	3	10
Cost error	1.50	50.00	2.25	3.50	45.00	0.50	2.00	5.00	25.50

First of all the data relating to the type of error was analysed. The data sorted into descending order and converted to percentages:

Table 15.3

	Error type								
	F	A	J	D	G	C	H	B	E
%	48.9	30.8	7.5	4.5	3.0	2.3	2.3	0.7	0.0

Next the data was plotted in graph form as a Pareto analysis chart to show the effect that error types F and A account for the greatest number of errors made on the invoices:

Fig. 15.2 Pareto analysis of error frequency in invoices

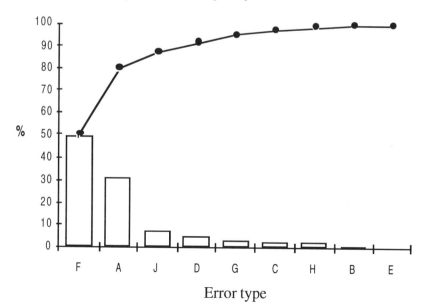

Error type

This Pareto analysis chart suggests that error types F and A should be investigated further. But the group first decided to investigate whether there was a Pareto pattern using different categories where they had also collected data. They analysed the cost of each error. From the data already gathered, the total cost for each error was calculated by multiplying the number of errors by the cost per error:

Table 15.4

	Error type								
	A	B	C	D	E	F	G	H	J
Total errors	41	1	3	6	0	65	4	3	10
Cost error	1.50	50.00	2.25	3.50	45.00	0.50	2.00	5.00	25.50
Total cost	61.50	50.00	6.75	21.00	0.00	32.50	8.00	15.00	255.00
%	13.7	11.00	1.5	4.7	0.0	7.2	1.8	3.3	56.7

The data was arranged in descending order and a new Pareto analysis chart on was produced:

Fig. 15.3 Pareto analysis of error frequency in invoices

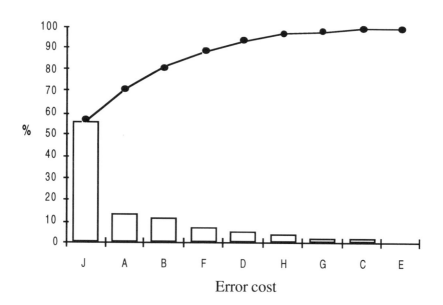

Error cost

This new analysis showed that errors J, A and B account for the majority of the costs of the errors. Whilst error J did not occur frequently, it accounted for the largest costs of all of the errors. If the group had only completed the first analysis, they would have investigated the most frequent error causes – the ones giving most customer irritation, but not the one that was causing the most cost to the company. By completing the second Pareto analysis the group was able to decide to investigate causes of error types J, A and F, tackling the error with the greatest cost benefits, and also the greatest frequency.

Pros and cons

Not all techniques are detailed and complex to use. Many are in everyday use and just need to be applied systematically in the problem solving process to be useful. This is the case with pro and con analysis. Everyone will have carried out this form of evaluation of a decision or options, consciously or unconsciously. Often, this is all that is required, especially when people want to make a quick decision and logic can be used to support that decision.

165

The activity should not need any specific guidance because it is such a familiar one. The idea is to keep a flow of rational choices on one side or the other on a chart or piece of paper. However, you should be aware of the temptation in pro and con listing to make a decision based on the total number of pros and cons rather than applying any weighting. It is worth remembering that if they are weighted as to importance, three pros can outweigh six cons or vice versa.

Fig. 15.4 Pro and con chart

PROS	CONS

Choice voting

Often, pro and con listing is not sufficiently detailed to make the decision clear, especially when there are deep seated opinions or feelings in the team that support or oppose one or more of the alternatives. Then a different form of analysis must be made to bring in the different opinions equally in the group. One of these techniques is Choice voting. It allows the choice to be made in such a way that the strength of everyone's personal preference is highlighted, and for this information to be used to make a decision.

First agree and write up the list of alternatives on a flipchart, checking that everyone understands the alternatives, and answering any points of clarification.

Next move to the voting. Allocate each individual member of the group ten points and ask them to allocate these points between the alternatives. The points can be allocated in whatever proportion they decide for themselves, and should reflect their strength of feeling about the alternatives. They can therefore allocate all ten points to one choice, or allocate one point between ten different choices, or any allocation between. The decision should be made in silence, so that there is no attempt to influence each other's voting, and the scores should be written down to ensure that the personal preference is recorded.

When everyone has put their scores next to the alternative choices, total each one and evaluate the results. The highest score will represent the preferred choice of the whole group. By looking at the alternatives where individuals allocated a high proportion of their ten points, a measure of the strength of personal preference for some of the alternatives can be achieved. If the highest overall score and the highest personal scores coincide, then the choice is clear. If, however, there are a significant number of the high personal scores allocated to another alternative which is not the overall choice, then some further discussion is required to resolve the differences. If no clear winner emerges, repeat the exercise limiting the options to the top three or four alternatives at the top of the voting in the first round.

Paired ranking

Paired ranking is another decision making method that helps to determine which option has the greatest benefit among several. Like Choice voting, it is particularly useful to measure personal preferences from a group of choices and measuring the amount of consensus in a group. It is a simple process of comparing each option with each other on a win:lose basis.

A Paired Ranking Matrix, as shown in Figure 15.5, is drawn up and each alternative is written in the boxes marked A, B, C, etc. The individual or the group vote on each comparison on a win:lose basis – the winning alternative gets 1 point, the losing alternative gets 0 points. Once the full sequence has been carried out, the scores are totalled and give a final rank order. If necessary the exercise can be repeated using the top few options to determine a clear winner.

Selection grid

Using a similar comparative voting system a Selection grid is a quick, yet accurate way of making a choice based on individual preference. It also introduces a step that promotes agreement and consensus on the criteria to be used in the decision.

167

Fig. 15.5 Paired ranking matrix

ITEM						
	A	**B**	**C**	**D**	**E**	**TOTAL**
A						
B						
C						
D						
E						

The construction of a Selection grid consists of two distinct operations – the agreement to the criteria to be used, and the completion and evaluation of the Selection grid. The criteria for the decision may be common for a number of different issues. It is important that the decision criteria should be chosen independently of knowledge of the options in order to maintain an objective standpoint. Some examples of criteria that are often used: benefit, ease to solve or to implement, time needed to solve or to implement, resources needed to solve or to implement, cost, probability of success, knowledge required to solve or to implement, personal preference, likelihood of support. (This is not an exhaustive list and should be used for guidance only.)

About five or six controlling criteria are required to evaluate the options. They determine what is important in making the choice. The Selection grid can then be drawn up with the options for the decision, as in Figure 15.6. The process works best when there are no more than eight options being considered at any one time. If the team wishes to compare more, then they should repeat the process several times, using the leading scores from each pass as the bench-marks to compare other options.

Each member considers each option against the criteria and gives points on a scale 1 to 5 (1 low, 5 high). This step should be done in silence in order to reduce interference and influence. After each individual has reached their personal scores, the points from all group members are recorded in the grid and the individual scores in each box in the grid added together. The boxes in the grid are then added across to give a total against each option.

As a further refinement, a numerical weighting can be assigned at the outset to each of the chosen criteria, showing the relative importance of each of the criteria in the decision process. The scores are then multiplied by the appropriate weighting to give a weighted total. This result will then reflect the relative importance of each of the criteria, and avoid the decision being influenced unduly by relatively unimportant criteria.

Fig. 15.6 Selection grid

Options	Decision criteria					TOTAL
	1	2	3	4	5	
1						
2						
3						
4						
5						

Clusters

Clusters is a technique that helps to organise information and ideas and promotes a deeper understanding of the problem that can lead to further insights and intuitive thoughts. In a group situation, clusters brings differences of perception and understanding within the group into the open where they can be assessed and discussed.

In analysing a problem or situation, people will often have an individual perception of the causes and factors involved. If these perceptions are too far apart, then problems in developing a clear analysis of the problem will develop, and solutions may not be effective. Therefore before making an attempt to solve a problem in these circumstances, a common understanding needs to be developed, with a collective insight and view as to the factors involved.

Clusters as an activity helps to develop this common understanding by its flexibility. The group write down the factors as they see them on self-adhesive notes, which are then stuck to a wall or other suitable flat surface. These notes can then be moved and clustered along with others to form a map of how the problem is perceived. By discussion and the rearrangement of the notes into other clusters and patterns a collective insight and understanding is developed. By using different coloured pens, each individual can keep track of her or his own input as the group picture is developed.

The process for Clusters is to give each person in the group a self-adhesive notepad and a coloured pen. Each member of the group writes down the factors they believe important, one factor on each note. These notes are randomly stuck them on a wall, white-board or table-top so that all can be seen, with sufficient space on the surface for more notes to be added, and for the notes to be moved around. Questions of clarification can be asked where necessary. The notes can be reworded at this time to add clarity, but not to change the meaning that was intended.

Once all the notes have been read, the group eliminates, by discussion and agreement all those where there is an obvious duplication. The replacement note is worded to combine the individual ideas, the original notes from the pattern are removed.

One member of the group then moves the notes around, to form them into a pattern which represents their view of the problem. Not all of the notes need be used, and they can be grouped together or positioned in any way which makes sense to the individual concerned. A commentary by the person explaining why certain choices are being made helps the rest of the group to follow her or his thinking process.

When one group member has developed a pattern, someone else takes over and reworks the pattern from how they see the problem. A commentary on why certain connections and moves are being made will start to identify the relative importance and differences that individuals will place on the problem factors.

With the whole group involved, some common factors will start to develop, and some of the clusters of notes can be combined into one or two broader descriptions to make handling easier. Major differences of perception can be discussed openly, and a common understanding of the problem will emerge. Often, as well as the common understanding, the process will develop some creative insights into the problem or situation which will facilitate the further development of solutions.

Although the process for Clusters is described above as a group activity, it is equally useful as an individual activity to help to organise data and information and to help to develop insights.

Fishbone diagram

When confronted with large amounts of data, one of the difficulties

Fig. 15.7 Examples of fishbone diagram ribs

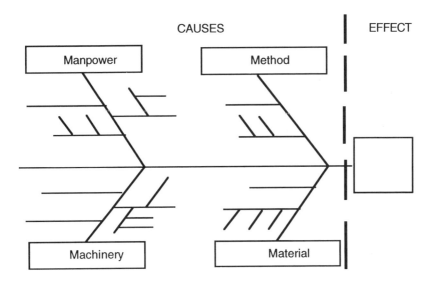

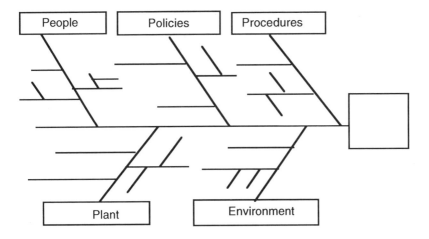

faced by individuals and teams in the Aim stage is to organise that data and separate causes from effects. In Japan, Kaoru Ishikawa developed a method of analysing problems which has become known as the cause and effect diagram, or Fishbone diagram, so called because when drawn, the diagram it resembles the skeleton of a fish. The Fishbone diagram ensures that the problem is properly analysed from all perspectives, and is viewed in its totality.

To make a Fishbone analysis, first obtain a large sheet of paper (flipchart-size paper in 'landscape' rather than 'portrait' mode is ideal). Write the problem on the right hand-side of the paper in a centred position. The problem should be stated in precise terms. The more general the problem statement or effect, the more general will be the causes generated. This problem statement is the 'Effect' from which the group will determine the possible causes.

Next draw in the main ribs of the fish, and write in the headings of the main problem areas. In most situations the main causes can be summarised under four main headings referred to as the 4 Ms: Manpower, Methods, Machinery and Materials. For problems more associated with administrative areas, the 4 Ps may be more helpful as main headings: Policies, Procedures, People and Plant. (These four main headings are only suggestions, some problems can be analysed with less than four headings. Some other problems may find the addition of other main ribs useful, e.g. environment.)

Then gather the causes information, writing each one down on the appropriate rib of the Fishbone. There is a choice of method here, either going round each rib in turn, or allowing freedom to brainstorm randomly. The latter method involves more agility by the writer, but is usually the more creative.

Main causes can be broken down further by branching out into subcauses on the skeleton. Go through each main cause in turn and ask 'Why does it happen?' and list the responses as branches off the main rib.

Finally analyse the diagram to isolate the most important causes and the ones that appear most frequently. This analysis will help to identify if more data needs to be gathered, or where potential solutions can be developed.

SWOT analysis

SWOT stands for Strengths, Weaknesses, Opportunities and Threats. This technique has already been used in Chapter 3 to help you to analyse the implications of your personal style and preferred roles. In the Aim stage, SWOT analysis can assist individuals or teams evaluate a situation or various options to determine the best course of action. By using the systematic process of analysis that a SWOT procedure provides, a thorough logical and rational evaluation can be achieved.

Fig. 15.8 A SWOT analysis chart

STRENGTHS	WEAKNESSES
OPPORTUNITIES	THREATS

Cost/Benefit analysis

In setting priorities and making decisions, the best option is often one that provides the most pay back for the least cost. When evaluating options therefore a cost/benefit analysis is a useful technique to apply.

Very simply, an estimate is made for each option in terms of its implementation cost and the likely returns or savings to be made. Different options can then be compared and the most effective pay-back can be followed through to implementation.

Like pro and con analysis, this may seem to be a natural activity, but if you have a strong bias towards Intuition, the relative merits of different solutions are not as important as the 'feel' that there is a right solution. Cost/benefit analysis can help to give further support to your intuition that will allow you to discuss the proposal with someone with a Sensing preference, or it can help you to check out your hunches and avoid costly errors. The benefit need not be measures in money terms. Other benefit values could be placed on the analysis (relationships, time, feelings, etc.) and measures made to evaluate the options.

Stakeholder mapping

Once a decision has been made on a solution or a strategy, then consideration also needs to be give to how the implementation might be organised. Several people or groups of people are likely to be affected. Stakeholder mapping will identify those people and form the basis on which you can develop an implementation strategy.

Some of these people will be those immediately affected, others will not be obvious, but could help or hinder the implementation plan if not considered. Stakeholder mapping is a group process that identifies all parties who have an involvement or who are affected by a particular change (the stakeholders) so that nothing is overlooked.

Figure 15.9 below shows a typical stakeholder map outline. The issue is written in the centre of a piece of paper and everyone affected are added to the chart. Names of individuals, jobs or groups of people are noted, the idea being to be inclusive rather than exclusive. Large groups can be broken down into their elements.

174

When the names have been added, some questions need to be posed: Who are the most important in terms of implementing the change? Who has to be involved? What harm could they do to the plan? Is there anyone who is an opinion leader who is key to the strategy? etc. The

Fig. 15.9 Example of a stakeholder map

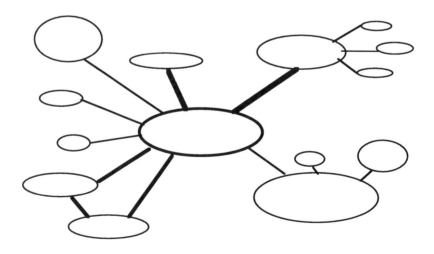

outcomes of these discussions can be graphically shown on the map by increasing the size of the line connecting the key people to the centre denoting strength and priority, by highlighting and clustering groups of people together who have similar objectives, etc.

The Stakeholder map can then be used as a guide to develop an action plan and implementation strategy.

Force field analysis

When implementing a change we often find that it is does not go as planned, and even that no progress at all is made. It seems that however hard we reason that the change is beneficial, an equal number of objections are raised which counteract our attempts to push forward.

This is the basis of a Force field – the forces that are helping drive the change are being met by forces which restrain or act against the change. The process of Force field analysis is designed to identify these forces in advance of the implementation of a desired change, and thus facilitate a more effective implementation strategy. A positive movement towards the change goal can be developed by reducing the restraining forces, add to or strengthening the driving forces, or both.

A Force field chart is very simply drawn by putting a vertical line down a flip chart, representing the equilibrium point. Directly above the line write up the current situation. Write the desired situation at the top right-hand corner. This then indicates the direction you wish the forces to take you. Label the left side of the page DRIVING FORCES, and the right side RESTRAINING FORCES.

The group process is to then list all of the forces working in favour of (driving) the change (drawing an arrow to indicate the direction of the force) and all the forces acting against (restraining) the change.

Once all of the main forces have been listed, then analyse the forces by adding some relative strengths to the forces – some will be stronger drivers or restrainers than others. The different strengths can be illustrated by drawing larger and smaller arrows

The Force field is now in equilibrium, the forces are equal on each side, and no movement is possible towards the desired change. In order to make it change to progress towards the desired outcome, then the restraining forces have to be reduced, the driving forces strengthened, or both. Experience has shown (along with Newton's Laws of Motion) that if the driving forces are increased there is a good possibility that an equal and opposite restraining effect will be produced. So the greatest benefit will derive from acting to reduce or eliminate the restraining forces.

To do this one first has to identify those forces than can be changed. Some will not be within the group member's control, so ignore these and brainstorm ways of overcoming or reducing the forces in their control.

Fig. 15.10 A force field chart

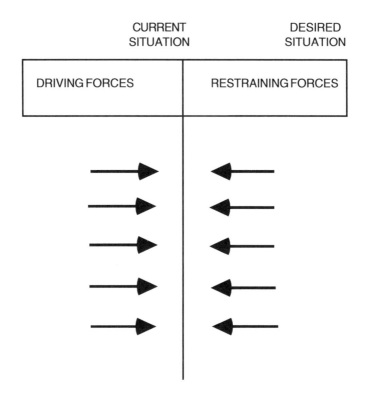

Potential problem analysis

Most plans and projects will not go strictly according to the plan, so it is worthwhile investing some time in thinking about what might go wrong so that contingencies can be drawn up. This activity assists people in looking at all the possibilities a project has for going wrong.

Working individually, list at least five items that might go wrong with the project and then gather them together. When the initial list has begun to reach completion, there are two options available, depending on the style of the team and the problem at hand. One option is to continue the analysis in a rational way and develop contingencies, the other way is to encourage people to go a step beyond and imagine what would happen if things went *really* wrong – what sorts of total disasters could occur?

Whether you have done a disaster analysis or a restricted problem analysis, the next steps are to begin making a list of what could be done to prevent the problems, and a list of the various things that need to be done to overcome the difficulty if it is encountered.

Table 15.5

POTENTIAL PROBLEM IDENTIFICATION

Disasters – What might go wrong?	How can we prevent them?	How can we overcome them?

Summary

The techniques for the Aim stage focus on the need to analyse the infomation gathered under the Ready stage. So they are concerned with organising data, evaluating options and setting priorities. Like any other techniques they are not a substitiute for the valuing of the stage or the process. They will help you in various stages of Aim to supplement your preferences and cover for gaps.

16

Developing 'Fire' skills and techniques

The 'Fire' stage in the problem solving process is all about getting things done, it is concerned with action and implementation. As we discussed in the earlier chapters on team roles, there are three-and-a-half roles that are associated with the Fire stage: Coordinator, Driver, Implementer and part of the Finisher role. We have also seen in the case studies on imbalanced organisations and teams that there is often a pressure to premature action that outweighs the dominance in numeric terms in the role balance. This pressure to move into action too early causes many of the problems with decision making. When working on individual problem solving projects, those who have relatively low scores on the Fire roles will also need to supplement your strengths in the other stages with action techniques that ensure you move ahead with care and decisiveness.

However, the propensity for teams to be biased towards action leads one to think that there would be little need to supplement or compensate for a lack of 'Fire power' by the use of techniques and activities. However, the absence of one or more of the important roles in the Fire stage can cause problems to a team that will need to be addressed by the whole team.

For instance, the key role of a Coordinator is to keep the team focused on the objective and process, and act as the chairman of the group. Without this role, the objectivity and focus of the team can be lost. The Driver gives shape and direction and is the task leader. Without this role the team can have a perfect plan but lack the leadership to carry it through effectively. The Implementer role gives the team the planning and scheduling ability to deal with complex implementation needs. In the absence of this role there can be a great deal of action that is un-coordinated and wasteful. Finally, the Finisher role ties up loose ends and completes the implementation of the task. Many teams and individuals leave these final steps undone with the result that further problems arise.

So, it is important that each of the Fire roles is represented in the action phase, otherwise the imbalance can destroy the most effective and creative decision or strategy devised by Ready – Aim. In this chapter, some techniques associated with each of these roles are outlined so that teams or individuals can use them to supplement the lack of inherent capability in their process. The techniques will also be of assistance to those who are relatively strong in the role and who wish to develop their skills or enhance the acceptance of their role in the team or organisation.

Table 16.1

'FIRE' TOOLS AND TECHNQUES

	Co-ordinating	Driving	Implementing	Finishing
HOW? – HOW? DIAGRAM	●		●	
WORK BREAKDOWN STRUCTURE	●		●	
GANTT CHARTS	●		●	
PERT CHARTS	●		●	
CRITICAL PATH ANALYSIS	●	●	●	●
SCHEDULE	●		●	●
CONTROL CHARTS	●			●
ACTION PLANS		●	●	●
ACTIVITY PLANS		●	●	●
CHAIRING A MEETING	●	●	●	
GENERATING ENTHUSIASM		●	●	

How? – How? diagram

This procedure is similar to the Why? – Why? diagram (see Chapter 15). The potential solution is analysed repeatedly by asking the question 'How?' until a complete picture of the practical implementation of that solution is reached. Different How? – How? diagrams can be created on different features of the solution and can then be compared and evaluated to determine the most appropriate implementation plan for the situation. An analysis of the diagram will also show up key implementation factors where greatest impact will be achieved.

As with the Why? – Why? process, the continual repetition of the question can become tedious unless the group works in a relaxed atmosphere. Also a large output is possible, requiring several sheets of flipchart paper, and a systematic process to keep account of the information.

The process is the same as for Why? – Why? diagrams – write the solution to be analysed centrally on the left-hand side of a flipchart and ask the group the question 'How?', recording all of the answers in the format shown in Figure 16.1.

After one round has been completed, take each of the answers to this round, and pose the question 'How?' again, and record the answers. Repeat this process asking 'How?' again and again until further answers become inappropriate. Use follow-on pages of flipchart paper to record the answers in flow chart format, pinning them to the wall so that they are all in view. Remember to number each page so that they can be retrieved and worked on in later sessions. These can be typed or stored in a computer if appropriate. Highlight Hows that are repeated more than once in the diagram, these represent the key elements in the implementation process.

Work breakdown structure

A work breakdown structure is a basic tool for the management and planning of any project or implementation activity. Following on the analysis carried out in a How? – How? diagram, it involves dividing the implementation into sub-units or work packages. By breaking down the work into sub-units at the earliest possible stage, you reduce the chances of neglecting or overlooking an essential step.

Start by identifying logical sub-divisions of the project, then break these down further until you reach the required detail. The amount of detail will depend on the complexity of the plan that you are implementing, but the aim should be to identify at least the packages of work, if not individual tasks. The systematic approach of identifying the major work packages and then moving to greater and greater detail until individual tasks and activities are identified will greatly reduce the common problem of missing out a key activity during the implementation stage due to the planning step being rushed. Drawing the breakdown in the form of a tree diagram, as in Figure 16.2 below, shows the relationship between the different tasks and elements and can give an overall picture of the plan with all of the pieces in place. It is at this stage that missing pieces are often spotted, saving costly errors and mistakes during the implementation period.

Once you have completed the main breakdown, you can then move on to produce detailed specifications and schedules that meet your quality, cost and time parameters.

Fig. 16.1 A How? – How? diagram outline

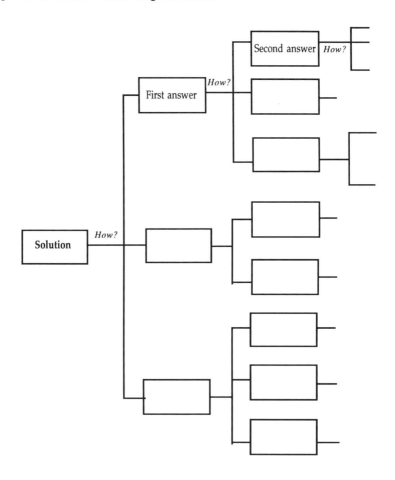

Fig. 16.2 Example of a work breakdown for an office re-organisation

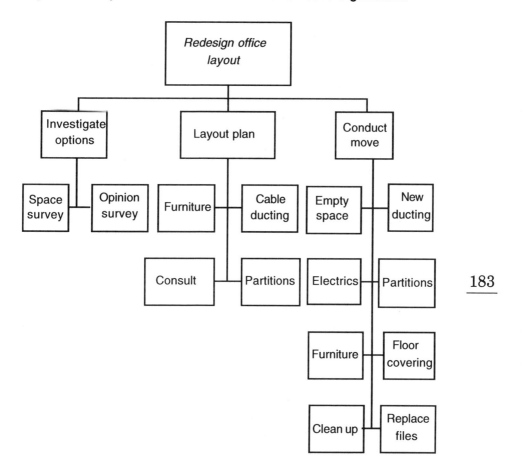

183

Gantt charts

Work breakdown and How? – How? processes help to define the needs
for the implementation plan, the next need is to put the plan into a
specific time frame. These are the two most commonly used methods
for charting the time element of a project are Gantt charts and PERT
charts, both of which are widely used in project management systems.
As a project is merely a number of activities that are linked together
over a period of time to achieve a single goal, the implementation of
almost every problem solving process can be seen as a project. Thus the

tools and techniques often pioneered by the major project management systems can be adapted and used in individual and team 'Fire' stages.

A Gantt chart is essentially a horizontal bar chart that is time based. It was first pioneered by Henry Gantt, the American industrial engineer, in the early 1900s. Their subsequent popularity derive from the ease of their construction and their interpretation. They are also easily adapted to a wide range of needs, and the increasing use of computer programs that carry out all of the detailed analysis and drawing work have allowed the technique to be accessible to a wide range of different applications and people. Being a visual representation of the plan on a detailed timetable, the progress of the implementation is clearly seen and can be tracked easily by everyone involved. As well as computer programs, several office equipment suppliers have their own kits and DIY bar chart systems that range from the very simple and flexible versions, often magnetic, to complex and more permanent styles using Lego style blocks.

Each step of a plan is represented by a horizontal bar on the chart. Steps that can be completed at the same time can occupy the same time segment, others must stay in sequence. The number of tasks and activities that can be completed simultaneously will depend on the resources available, so the completion of a Gantt chart begins to reflect the true nature of the plan, rather than the broad estimates or hopes that may have been expressed at the point of decision.

To draw a Gantt chart estimate the time required for each step in your work breakdown, then draw on to a grid, bearing in mind the sequence of events. Once again, the use of computer models or proprietary systems allow the chart to be manipulated easily depending on the resources available, and the implications of different patterns are clearly seen.

PERT charts

The other main form of project planning chart that plots the activity schedule against time is the PERT chart. PERT stands for Programme Evaluation and Review Technique. It is a more sophisticated form of planning than the Gantt charts, and is useful when there are many interactive steps in the project as it shows the relationship between steps and activities in a more graphic manner.

The three components of a PERT diagram are 'events' that are represented by circles; 'activities' that are represented by arrows connecting

Fig. 16.3 Example of a Gantt chart

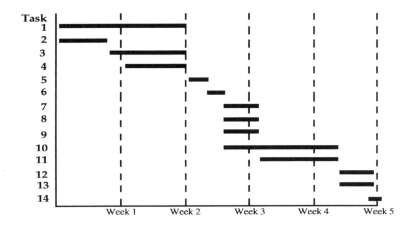

Fig. 16.4 Example of a PERT CHART

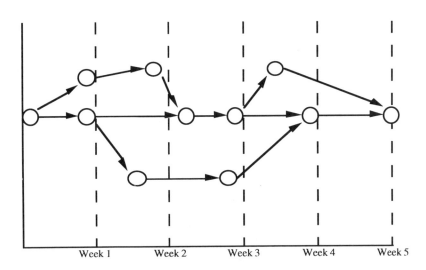

the circles; and 'non-activities' (a dependency where no work is required) connecting two events shown by dotted line arrows.

To draw a PERT diagram, you follow a similar process to a Gannt chart, again estimating the time to complete each step on the work breakdown. The difference comes in that the relationships need to be identified and a correct sequence of activities established. The PERT chart is then drawn as a network of relationships among the steps showing the proper sequencing. Steps that can be undertaken at the same time are shown on different paths. The length of the lines between events shows the time needed for the activity, and the critical measurement points are clearly shown as the junctions between different pathways. The longest path through the network identifies the essential steps that must be completed on time to avoid a delay in the project schedule.

Critical path analysis

The PERT chart is one way of graphically representing a critical path through the implementation of the project. One of the difficulties encountered with a Gantt chart is that it does not indicate the interdependence between the individual tasks. So when implementing a plan, a delay in completion of one task may not be serious in terms of the overall completion timing if it does not hinder the completion of other tasks. However, if tasks cannot be started until one or more other tasks are complete (for example, the roof of a house cannot be started until the walls have been built), then a delay is a critical factor in the overall completion of the project.

So that greater control could be exercised over projects, especially where there were critical sequence issues, the simple bar chart was further developed into Critical Path Analysis. This process became popular after spectacular improvements in the planning and control of defence-related projects in the USA in the 1950s. Although pioneered for large and complex projects, the process is equally valid for small-scale operations where there is a logical dependency between different jobs and activities.

In constructing a critical path, the relationship between activities must be examined and any dependencies notes. Then these are drawn out, usually on an arrow diagram similar to a PERT chart but without the time parameter added. This then shows the sequencing and critical tasks for the implementation plan. For simple plans this may be all that is required, for more complex projects the timings can be added and a full PERT chart drawn.

Figure 16.5 below shows a simple dependency diagram, event 6 cannot be started until event 5 is complete, which in its turn is dependent on the previous activities being completed. The critical path is the shortest possible line drawn through the dependent activities. It is this path that need to be carefully monitored in order to keep the implementation on schedule.

Fig. 16.5 Example of a cricial relationship

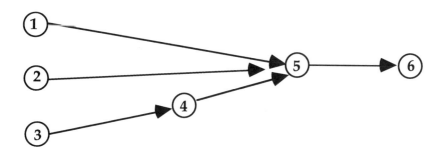

Schedules

Using the work breakdown, and Gantt and PERT processes and critical path analysis as appropriate, a schedule can be drawn up. This document details the critical path of the project, the time and cost factors and the allocation of resources and acts as a control document during implementation. These schedule summaries provide the basic inputs to action plans and activity plans that are essential for ensuring completion and control of an implementation plan.

Control charts

Once an implementation is under way, there is a need to ensure that each event is recorded and controlled. A status check on the budget and schedule provides a good reference point for this control activity and highlights variances from the plan that may need corrective action. Other parameters for control other than cost and schedule can be used depending on the nature of the project and the critical success factors for the implementation. The process, however, remains the same – maintaining a regular check to make sure activities are finished to specification and within the parameters laid down in the plan.

Table 16.2

EXAMPLE OF AN IMPLEMENTATION SCHEDULE

PROJECT: REDESIGN OFFICE LAYOUT			
Step	**Budget**	**Schedule**	**Responsibility**
Opinion survey	£300	3 days	Jim
Space survey	£250	*1 day	Angela
Plan layout	£300	2 days	Jim
Design cable ducting	£150	1 day	Jim
Choose furniture	£250	*2 days	Angela
Layout partitions	£100	1 day	Jim
Consult staff	£200	1 day	Jim
Empty space	£1,000	1 day	Bob
Install ducting	£2,500	3 days	Bob
Install electrics	£1,000	2 days	Bob
Floor covering	£1,250	1 day	Bob
Install furniture	£4,000	1 day	Angela
Clean up	£250	0.5 day	Bob
Replace files	£1,000	1 day	Bob
Total	**£12,550**	**20.5 days**	

*Not on critical path

Fig. 16.6 Example of a control chart

TASK	COST				SCHEDULE			
	Budget	Actual	Variance	Total	Planned	Actual	Variance	Total

Action plans

As the name implies, action plans are summaries of what action needs to be taken to complete a task or work schedule. They detail the outcome expected, the activity detail, who is responsible and other important control parameters such as cost and time. Use of action plans help team members to see their own responsibilities and supplement the need for finishing control on the tasks in the critical path.

Activity plans

Activity plans are similar in some ways to action plans, but their main purpose is to summarise activities of one person or department rather than by task activity which is the strength of the action plan. The objective is the same, to ensure that the planned activities are carried out according to plan, and to ensure that everyone involved in the plan understands her or his own activities and expectations.

Fig. 16.7 Example of an action plan

Project				
Goal or target				
Measures of success:				
Steps/Actions	Responsibility		Resource	Timeframe

Fig. 16.8 Example of an activity plan

ACTIVITY LIST						
Name						
Activity		Schedule		Estimate		
		Start	Finish	Hours	Materials	Expense

Chairing a meeting

One of the prime functions of a Coordinator is to co-ordinate the actions of a group of people in a meeting. The original term used by Belbin in his research for this role was Chairman, though this has been changed due to the confusion of the position with the role. The role is an essential part of the team, but the functions need not be carried out by the chairperson or leader (though it helps if the co-ordinator has some positional power as well). If there is not a Coordinator in the team, then the probability will be that the team meetings will not be well organised or objective. In an individual situation, the skills of chairing a meeting apply to the objective approach of organising information and ordering items in a work breakdown or planning system.

What is a meeting? We often view a meeting as a group of people sitting round a table, discussing items on an agenda and making decisions – a boardroom-type of meeting. These meetings are fairly formal in their style and are under the control of a chairman. They have appointed functional roles such as secretary, minute taker and often have sub-committees and formal reports.

Many other meetings resemble the formal, structured events, but are not structured and seem to wander from item to item with no plan or logical flow. Actions and agreements are not recorded and no one seems to be prepared for the discussion that takes place. Then there are the informal discussions and conversations between two or more people that fill up the rest of the working day.

In fact, all of these can constitute a meeting. They are all occasions when a group of people pool some ideas or share information. It means that the vast majority of a normal working day for most managers is spent (or misspent) in meetings. The problem with most meetings is that no one has planned for the activity or pulls the disparate items together. Very often no one recognises that a meeting is taking place. No one is taking on the co-ordinating or leading role. The meeting becomes no more than a gathering of people.

Establish a purpose

The first step necessary to take control of these gatherings and make them into effective and efficient meetings is to establish a purpose for the meeting. Whether it is a telephone call, a committee meeting, a board meeting, a management meeting or, in the context of this book, a problem solving meeting, there must be a focus, an objective. What is the meeting aiming to achieve? What are the outcomes that are expected? How can I judge whether it has been a success or a failure? What would be the effect if the meeting was not held?

By asking these questions, a large number of potentially time wasting meetings can be avoided. Many meetings would never simply never take place and a vast number of other meetings would cease to happen. The time saving would be immense if all of the regular meetings that have been etched into the daily, weekly and monthly schedules of most organisations are subjected to the scrutiny of defining their purpose. Many will have had a purpose at one time, but custom and practice will have long since taken over and the original need lost in the past.

Meetings in organisations tend to fall into three or four main categories: information sharing, problem solving, decision making, or implementation control are the most common. This gives a function for the meeting, the next step is to determine the precise objective or objectives for the meeting that you are planning to run or attend.

193

Preparation

Once it has been established that there is a need for the meeting, the next task in the co-ordination process is to plan and prepare for the meeting. Once again, a massive amount of time is wasted in meetings due to a lack of planning and preparation, the central tool of which is the agenda.

The agenda gives structure to the objective and ensures that the purpose of the meeting is fulfilled. An agenda is not just a list of topics for discussion; it should be a detailed explanation of the objective and expected outcome of each item, the time allocation for the item, the people who need to contribute and the process to be used (for instance: round-table discussion, agreement to a previously circulated paper, open discussion, brainstorming session, etc.). If a detailed agenda is produced, each individual team member can prepare appropriately for the meeting and the contributions will therefore be more effective. It is even possible for people to plan to attend for the part of the meeting that concerns them and not have to sit through interminable debate waiting for their five minute slot.

The chairman or leader should not be afraid of producing a long agenda, provided that it is composed of useful information and defines each item appropriately, and is not just a long list of items that are more than the time allowed will accommodate. Use of phrases like 'for discussion', 'for information', 'for decision' help to focus the planning and involvement of participants.

Supporting papers should always be included with the agenda. These add further detail to the agenda item and help participants to prepare for the meeting. Otherwise time is wasted by people reading background papers at the meeting and not having time to prepare their inputs and comments.

Whilst agendas only seem to be important for formal meetings, they are of immense value to informal meetings as well. To consider the purpose and objective of the discussion, the state of preparation of the other participants and what they need to know in advance of the discussion, and the expected outcome will radically improve even the smallest meeting. Whilst the agenda need not be formally circulated and written down, a call or pre-discussion to set the ground rules and agree the agenda and outcomes is often a great time and effort saver.

Timing

The final, and most important step in drawing up an agenda is to ensure that it is correctly ordered. Just like a critical path analysis, there is a logical flow to most meetings, where some decisions are dependent on others. The agenda needs to reflect this order to be effective. It may also be possible to sequence the agenda so as to limit the time spent by participants who are not required for the whole of the meeting. By scheduling their attendance at the beginning or at the end of the meeting, and putting all items that concern them together, the disruption to the meeting is limited and the disruption to individuals' time is also limited.

Another timing consideration in setting the agenda and running the meeting is to consider where the time wasting occurs. Often this is in the 'catch-all' item of 'Any Other Business'. There will always be some urgent item that has arisen since the agenda has been circulated, but the use of the Any Other Business agenda item is often a cover for a lack of planning. Items should be part of the main agenda whenever possible. To avoid some of the temptations of the Any Other Business item, one control mechanism is to put it at the beginning of the agenda. You then avoid the time wasting discussion on a subject that has been triggered by discussion during the meeting, but is not urgent and is unimportant for this meeting.

The beginning of a meeting is likely to be more creative and full of energy than the end of a meeting, so the scheduling of discussions needing mental energy are best at the start of an agenda.

Starting and finishing times are obligatory for the whole meeting, and it is often a good discipline to time individual items as well. This way the team can share in the responsibility of keeping to time.

Administrative arrangements

The agenda is the most important planning tool for a successful meeting, but the co-ordination activity also involves some practical actions to ensure that the meeting will run smoothly. The following checklist will assist in ensuring that everything is covered:

Fig. 16.9 Meeting checklist

❏ Room booked
❏ Enough seats and space
❏ Additional rooms for small group discussions
❏ Cateriing
❏ Power sockets and public address
❏ Presentation equipment
  – Flipchart easel and paper
  – Overhead projector
  – White-board
  – Screen
  – Marker pens
  – Slide/film projector
  – Video
  – Spare bulbs
  – Masking tape/Blu-Tack
  – Other
❏ Participant requirements
  – Paper and pens
  – Water and glasses
  – Name cards
  – Message board
  – Secretarial services
❏ Agenda prepared and circulated
❏ Papers circulated
❏ Participants advised
❏ Roles agreed

Controlling the discussion

Most agendas and agenda items have a logical flow to them. First establish the need and collect information on the subject, then analyse the data and come to a diagnosis or decision before agreeing on a course of action. It is the Ready – Aim – Fire process in miniature. If the matter is complex, then the process may be spread over several meetings, and other techniques for participation, as discussed in this and earlier chapters, can be employed to aid the discussion.

Controlling the discussion means looking at two areas – the subject and the people. The subject is covered by the agenda planning and the Ready – Aim – Fire process. So long as the chairman or leader keeps in mind the logical flow of Ready – Aim – Fire and the purposes of the agenda item and meeting, the discussion should stay on track. In groups where there is a particularly strong bias away from the logical and systematic approach, the chairman may need to break the discussion down into very small segments, writing the stages upon a flipchart to keep everyone informed of the road map for the meeting. As stated earlier, however, one of the key needs is to show some value to the process to convince those with different perceptions that following the ground rules is of benefit. It is therefore also important for the chairman or leader to consider the people side of the meeting.

Knowing the personal preferences and roles of the team members is the essential first step in controlling the people side of the meeting. Sharing this information among the participants also shares the responsibility for ensuring that the discussion follows some agreed guidelines. The chairman is all too often unfairly castigated for the lack of control of meetings. She or he does bear part of the burden, but as most have never received any training for the position, and most will be given the role due to their seniority rather than any skill in the function, shouldering the total blame for ineffective meetings ignores the others who are equally responsible – the participants.

All of the points so far made for the chairman or leader to take responsibility for can be equally shared by the other participants. For instance: the chairman has a decision to make regarding who should be present, equally each participant has a responsibility to question whether they need to attend or not; the chairman draws up the agenda, the participants should ensure that it is received and understood; the chairman plans the process and guides the meeting, the participants have a responsibility to follow the agreed process. So in controlling the meeting, if there is a lack of skill in the co-ordinating and driving roles, the team should agree to follow the ground rules together and share the responsibility, not appoint one person to be the scapegoat.

In meetings there are different personalities that can cause disruption and an ineffective use of time: the strong and the weak, the talkative and the silent. Depending on the personalities involved in the meeting, you may need to agree a process that ensures everyone has an equal opportunity to contribute. An agenda is the first step in all of these different processes, ensuring that everyone gets the opportunity to plan their contribution. To control discussion an allow an equal say, a round-table process works well, but may be inefficient in time management as it allows everyone to have an opportunity to speak, even if they have not real contribution to make. Again, individual responsibility helps the process work well.

Seniority often goes hand in hand with meeting chairing or leading. This causes a double problem for the more junior participants, especially in a controversial situation – to contribute they need to confront the positional power of the chairperson of the meeting and the positional power of their senior. It is therefore a good idea to confront the tradition that the senior person present takes the chair, and allocate the chair to the most skilled or the most appropriate for the stage of the discussion. In the latter situation, the best person to chair an evaluation session would be someone who has one of the Aim roles; the best person to run a creative thinking session would be someone with one of the Ready roles. In any event, the senior person does not have to take the chair, and can probably contribute more effectively from the body of the meeting as an equal participant.

197

A final point to consider when looking to control a meeting is that it is possible to bring in a professional, impartial chairperson from outside the group to do the job. Many boards of directors already do this by appointing an Non-executive Chairman to oversee the board meetings. The same can be applied to other meetings – separating the task interest from the role of the chair can radically improve the discussion and decision making. Many companies are now using their own staff or consultants as meeting facilitators – responsible for the effective running of the meeting process, allowing the participants to focus all of their attention on the task content.

Recording the outcomes

Action plans and agreements from meetings need to be recorded so that everyone is in possession of the same record of outcomes. Even in the best-run meeting, the difference in perception of the individual members will mean that everyone will have a slightly different memory of the discussion and the agreed actions. It is therefore important that agreements be written down, ideally at the time, and that actions agreed are recorded with the name of the person responsible and the expected outcomes. These minutes or action plans need not be long. Verbatim records of discussion have a place in the courtroom, rarely in a business meeting. The essential meeting minutes should record the purpose of the agenda item, if necessary a brief record of the discussion points, the decision reached and the action agreed on, with names and times agreed.

The lack of such records can cause endless delays and misunderstandings and waste time at future meetings while the team tries to agree on what was agreed before. Along with some colleagues, I have recently been associated with helping to start up business operations in Eastern Europe. Here there has been a long tradition of meetings and discussion, but coupled very often with a lack of action. Discussion at one planning meeting in St Petersburg was easy when problems were being aired, information gathered and agreements made on what needed to be done. The next step of drawing up an action plan with the names of the managers responsible for seeing the item through proved the stumbling block. No one would agree to have their name recorded against a particular item. Everyone agreed to the need for action, and everyone agreed that if someone did not take the responsibility to follow that action through, nothing would get done. But no one would take that responsibility. The historical culture in Russia and the Soviet Union was that the only need for someone to be personally identified with a project was so that there was someone to blame when it went wrong. Consequently, even in a more positive environment, there was a reluctance to be personally identified. As a consequence it took as long to redecorate the canteen at the St Petersburg factory as it did to build a completely new factory on a greenfield site in Turkey. The importance of action planing and having clear agreements and responsibilities for seeing them through is clear.

Generating enthusiasm

The gap that is made in a team by the absence of a Driver in the Fire stage is often one of enthusiasm – the drive associated with the role title is missing. The Driver often has a holistic view of what is being achieved, and is future as well as action oriented. The Driver often has a vision of what will be achieved, without necessarily knowing the steps to take to get there. A vision for success in the team project is one way to generate enthusiasm and cover for the lack of a driving force in the team.

A clear and shared vision of achievement in the future is a powerful guide and motivator. It is like planting an anchor in the future with the anchor chain feeding back over time to the present. We can then hold on to that anchor chain and pull on it or wind it in to get us closer and closer to our goal. The anchor provides the stability to get us past obstacles and strong currents that try to push us off course. Knowing that we can get there is a powerful driver to action.

Visioning and visualising success is a technique that has been employed by successful sportsmen and women for years. The pre-race preparation of a 100 metre sprinter, the marathon runner, the downhill skier or the tennis player is geared to focusing the mind on the finish and on winning the race. An intense mental preparation takes place with a concentration that blocks out all other influences of the crowd, other competitors and the environment. Very often you see images of athletes on television with their eyes closed, mentally rehearsing each stage of the race. Skiers can be observed making the movements of their body around each curve of the track before they put on their skis. Tennis players learn the technique of concentrating on where the ball is going to land rather than how to hit it. Golfers are regularly seen playing practice air shots around the green – in the words of the commentators 'getting the feel of the shot'.

All of these techniques can be applied to team situations as well as individual competition – the step that is required is that the vision and feelings have to be shared, not kept to oneself. Sports teams manage to do this with their frequent practice and rehearsal sessions, their coaching of each other, and their game plans for success. But just like individual sports where there is little transfer of our experience that continual learning and practice is necessary to achieve and maintain success, so the team success approach is rarely transferred to the business environment. We will happily go out each week and practise our golf swing or our tennis stroke, and even pay for regular tuition, but we rarely seek out practice and training at work. We train with our sports teams on a regular basis and take time to develop a plan for the game and rehearse moves, but we rarely plan for meetings at work or take time out to rehearse possible moves and to play to each others strengths.

Charles Handy in his book *The Empty Raincoat* describes the typical British work team being like a rowing eight 'eight people going backwards as fast as they can, without talking to each other, commanded by the one person who can't row'.[1] He goes on to point out that he then learned the truth about rowing from an oarsman who explained that they could only develop the confidence to go backwards without talking and be led by a non-rower by the long periods where they live together, eat together and practise together. The typical work team did not resemble the rowing eight, as it attempted to carry out a similar role without the time spent in practice and off-the-job time.

To avoid some of these faults, the team can first be turned round to face the way they are going. A clear, shared vision of the future will enable everyone to focus on the objectives and look forwards rather than backwards. But visions are of no use unless they are built on firm foundations. They need the solid common ground of shared values and beliefs on which to grow. Without shared values, the vision is merely a dream or a fantasy. It must be taken seriously for any progress to be made.

So, the actions that you can take as an individual or in a team to engender some enthusiasm and direction in the implementation project is to establish some common values and beliefs 'what we all want to achieve'. 'what we all believe in', 'what we have in common' and then build a vision of success 'what it will be like when we achieve the plan'. Establish your anchor in the future and pull on the chain to get you there as quickly as possible. Spend the time with your team in off the job activities to help to share experiences and values and practise co-operation and teamwork. Share your perceptions, preferences and roles to ensure a greater understanding and valuing of each other's place in the team, building the common ground that you can then use to develop further visions of success.

Summary

Techniques for the Fire stage are all about planning and scheduling and getting things done. To be effective in a team environment, you need to be able to chair or lead a meeting and to generate enthusiasm and drive for your project. You also need to be able to break down the work into individual tasks and to schedule and control work in progress. Finally you need to finish things off. The skills of project management (see Chapter 12) are very appropriate to this stage of problem solving.

[1] Charles Handy, *The Empty Raincoat*, Random House, 1994.

17

Conclusion

As I said in the introduction, this book is about understanding yourself and valuing others. By analysing your personal preferences and by understanding and valuing other perceptions and processes, you will be able to use a balanced approach to problem solving that will enable you to make the best use of the people and resources available, and make more effective decisions. The exercises and activities are only the tip of an iceberg of techniques for self-development. Application to the real-life situations that surround you reflections on your learnings and experience will enhance your understanding of the process and identify needs for further development. Apprndix 2 contains some suggestions for further reading.

I hope that this book has provided one small step in the development of a balanced viewpoint and in the development of a decision making process that is more based on information rather than prejudice and opinion.

Appendix 1
A self-perception inventory

∎

Directions

For each section distribute a total of ten points among the sentences which you think best describe your behaviour. These points may be distributed among several sentences: in extreme cases they might be spread among all the sentences or ten points may be given to a single sentence. Enter the points in the table at the end of the inventory.

I What I believe I can contribute to a team:

(a) I think I can quickly see and take advantage of new opportunities.

(b) I can work well with a very wide range of people.

(c) Producing ideas is one of my natural assets.

(d) My ability rests in being able to draw people out whenever I detect they have something of value to contribute to group objectives.

(e) My capacity to follow through has much to do with my personal effectiveness.

(f) I am ready to face temporary unpopularity if it leads to worthwhile results in the end.

(g) I am quick to sense what is likely to work in a situation with which I am familiar.

(h) I can offer a reasoned case for alternative courses of action without introducing bias or prejudice.

II If I have a possible shortcoming in teamwork, it could be that:

(a) I am not at ease unless meetings are well structured and controlled and generally well conducted.

(b) I am inclined to be too generous towards others who have a valid viewpoint that has not been given a proper airing.

(c) I have a tendency to talk a lot once the group gets on to new ideas.

(d) My objective outlook makes it difficult for me to join in readily and enthusiastically with colleagues.

(e) I am sometimes seen as forceful and authoritarian if there is a need to get something done.

(f) I find it difficult to lead from the front, perhaps because I am overresponsive to group atmosphere.

2 (g) I am apt to get too caught up in ideas that occur to me and so lose track of what is happening.

(h) My colleagues tend to see me as worrying unnecessarily over detail and the possibility that things may go wrong.

III When involved in a project with other people:

4 (a) I have an aptitude for influencing people without pressurising them.

2 (b) My general vigilance prevents careless mistakes and omissions being made.

(c) I am ready to press for action to make sure that the meeting does not waste time or lose sight of the main objective.

2 (d) I can always be counted on to contribute something original.

(e) I am always ready to back a good suggestion in the common interest.

1 (f) I am keen to look for the latest in new ideas and developments.

\ (g) I believe my capability for cool judgement is appreciated by others.

(h) I can be relied upon to see that all essential work is organised.

IV My characteristic approach to group work is that:

(a) I have a quiet interest in getting to know colleagues better.

(b) I am not reluctant to challenge the views of others or to hold a minority view myself.

(c) I can usually find a line of argument to refute unsound propositions.

2 (d) I think I have a talent for making things work once a plan has been put into operation.

((e) I have a tendency to avoid the obvious and to come out with the unexpected.

3 (f) I bring a touch of perfectionism to any team job I undertake.

(g) I am ready to make use of contacts outside the group itself.

4 (h) While I am interested in all of the views I have no hesitation in making up my mind once a decision has to be made.

V I gain satisfaction in a job because:

3 (a) I enjoy analysing situations and weighing up all the possible choices.

203

(b) I am interested in finding practical solutions to problems.

(c) I like to feel I am fostering good working relationships.

(d) I can have a strong influence on decisions.

(e) I can meet people who may have something new to offer.

(f) I can get my people to agree on a necessary course of action.

(g) I feel in my element where I can give a task my full attention.

(h) I like to find a field that stretches my imagination.

VI If I am suddenly given a difficult task with limited time and unfamiliar people:

(a) I would feel like retiring to a corner to devise a way out of the impasse before developing a line.

(b) I would be ready to work with the person who showed the most positive approach, however difficult he might be.

(c) I would find some way of reducing the size of the task by establishing what different individuals might best contribute.

(d) My natural sense of urgency would help to ensure that we did not fall behind schedule.

(e) I believe I would keep cool and maintain my capacity to think straight.

(f) I would retain a steadiness of purpose in spite of the pressures.

(g) I would be prepared to take a positive lead if I felt the group was making no progress.

(h) I would open up discussions with a view to stimulating new thoughts and getting something moving.

VII With reference to the problems to which I am subject in working in groups:

(a) I am apt to show my impatience with those who are obstructing progress.

(b) Others may criticise me for being too analytical and insufficiently intuitive.

(c) My desire to ensure that work is propoerly done can hold up proceedings.

(d) I tend to get bored rather easily and rely on one or two stimulating members to spark me off.

(e) I find it difficult to get started unless the goals are clear.

(f) I am sometimes poor at explaining and clarifying complex points that occur to me.

(g) I am conscious of demanding from others the things I cannot do myself.

(h) I hesitate to get my points across when I run up against real opposition.

Points table for self-perception inventory

Section	Item							
	a	b	c	d	e	f	g	h
I	1	3	2	1	2			1
II		3	5				2	
III	4	2		2	7	1	1	
IV				2	1	3		4
V	2	1	2	1	1	1	1	1
VI	1	3	2			1	2	2
VII	1					3	4	2

To interpret the self-perception inventory you should now look at the analysis sheet that follows.

Self-perception inventory analysis sheet

Transpose the scores taken from the points table above, entering them section by section in the table below. Then add up the points in each column to give a total team role distribution score.

Section	A	B	C	D	E	F	G	H
I	g 1	d 3	f 2	c 1	a 2	h	b	e 1
II	a	b 3	e 5	g	c	d	f 2	h
III	h 4	a 2	c	d 2	f 1	g 1	e 1	b
IV	d	h	b	e 2	g 1	c 3	a	f 4
V	b 2	f 1	d 2	h 1	e 1	a 1	c 1	g 1
VI	f 1	c 3	g 2	a	h	e	b 2	d 2
VII	e 1	g	a	f	d	b 3	h 4	c 2
Total	9	12	11	6	4	8	10	10

Source: R. Meredith Belbin, *Management Teams: Why They Succeed or Fail* (Butterworth Heinemann, 1981). Reproduced with permission.

206

The eight team roles

	Names used in this book	Original Belbin names[1]	Current Belbin names[2]
A	**IMPLEMENTER**	COMPANY WORKER	IMPLEMENTER
B	**COORDINATOR**	CHAIRMAN	COORDINATOR
C	**DRIVER**	SHAPER	SHAPER
D	**CREATOR**	PLANT	PLANT
E	**INVESTIGATOR**	RESOURCE INVESTIGATOR	RESOURCE INVESTIGATOR
F	**EVALUATOR**	MONITOR EVALUATOR	MONITOR EVALUATOR
G	**COMMUNICATOR**	TEAMWORKER	TEAMWORKER
H	**FINISHER**	COMPLETER FINISHER	COMPLETER

207

[1] R. Meredith Belbin, *Management Teams: Why They Succeed or Fail*, Butterworth Heinemann, 1981
[2] R. Meredith Belbin, *Team Roles at Work*, Butterwoth Heinemann, 1993

Appendix 2
Further development and reading

■

A list of books and references for those of you who wish to explore further some of the development activities referred to in this book:

Personal style

David Keirsey and Marilyn Bates, *Please Understand Me* (Prometheus Nemesis Books, 1978)

David Keirsey, *Portraits of Temperament* (Prometheus Nemesis Books, 1987)

Stephone Montgomery, *The Pygmalion Project*, Vols 1–4 (Prometheus Nemesis Books, 1989)

R. Craig Hogan and David W. Champagne, *Personal Style Inventory* (Organisation Design & Development, 1979; available in the UK through Management Learning Resources, Carmarthen)

Teams:

R. Meredith Belbin, *Management Teams - Why They Succeed or Fail* (Heinemann, 1981)

R. Meredith Belbin, *Team Roles at Work* (Heinemann, 1993)

Kenneth Blanchard, Donald Carew and Eunice Parisi-Carew, *The One Minute Manager Builds High Performing Teams* (HarperCollins, 1990)

Jon R. Katzenbach and Douglas K. Smith, *The Wisdom of Teams* (Harvard Business School Press, 1993)

Creative thinking and problem solving

Geof Cox, Chuck Dufault and Walt Hopkins, *50 Activities on Creativity and Problem Solving* (Connaught Training, 1991)

Roger van Oech, *A Whack on the Side of the Head* (Warner Books, 1993)

Edward de Bono, *I Am Right, You Are Wrong* (Viking Books, 1990)

Balanced process/valuing different perspectives

Roger Fisher and William Ury, *Getting to Yes* (Hutchison, 1982)

Roger Fisher and Scott Brown, *Getting Together* (Century Hutchison, 1989)

Charles Handy, *The Empty Raincoat – Making Sense of the Future* (Random House, 1994)

Charles Handy, *The Age of Unreason* (Century Hutchison, 1989)

Peter Block, *The Empowered Manager* (Josey-Bass, 1987)

Anita Roddick, *Body and Soul* (Ebury Press, 1991)

Tom Peters and Nancy Austin, *A Passion for Excellence* (Random House, 1985)

Richard Pascale, *Managing on the Edge* (Penguin Books, 1990)

Index

■

213